Don't Move—
Improve!

An Owl Book

Henry Holt and Company

New York

DON'T MOVE-
IMPROVE!

52 Home-Enhancement Projects

That Can Be Completed in One Weekend or less

KATIE and GENE HAMILTON

Published by Henry Holt and Company, Inc.,
115 West 18th Street, New York, New York 10011.
Published in Canada by Fitzhenry & Whiteside Limited,
91 Granton Drive, Richmond Hill, Ontario, L4B 2N5.
ISBN 0-8050-1378-4
Book Design by Claire Naylon Vaccaro
Illustrations by Jackie Aher
Printed in the United States of America

We'd like to dedicate this book to some special people in our lives who've become good friends. We want to thank all of our editors at the home and workshop magazines who've helped us develop the craft of how-to writing.

Our sincere thanks go to editor Theresa Burns who has worked fast and furiously to help this book take shape and to Jane Jordan Browne who continues to be our good friend and agent.

We're grateful for the help we received from sewing expert Sandy Bemis. Our gratitude also extends to Claire Naylon Vaccaro, who designed this book, and Jackie Aher, who illustrated it.

Contents

CHAPTER THREE: CREATIVE WAYS WITH WINDOWS AND WALLS

CHAPTER FOUR: KITCHEN AND BATHROOM MAGIC

CHAPTER FIVE: DOABLE DOOR AND CEILING PROJECTS

CHAPTER SIX: MORE-ROOM-THAN-YOU-THOUGHT PROJECTS

CHAPTER SEVEN: ENERGY-SAVING IDEAS

CHAPTER EIGHT: EASY-TO-DO HOME ELECTRONICS PROJECTS

CHAPTER NINE: PROJECTS FOR THE GREAT OUTDOORS

Introduction

Staying put and making improvements to the house you have makes a lot of sense when you compare it to the expense, frustration, and disruption of moving. It's especially true when your family has put down roots in a neighborhood. So, the house isn't exactly perfect; there are plenty of projects that you can do to improve it without spending a lot of time and money.

Now, don't say you're not handy. You don't have to have been born with a chisel or paintbrush in your hand to make your house something beautiful and uniquely your own. Rarely are handy homeowner skills inherited at birth. You get them the old-fashioned way—by earning them one project at a time.

With fourteen renovated houses and our twenty-fifth wedding anniversary behind us, there's one piece of advice that we both agree on: *Make your first home-fix-up projects attainable*. If you can't complete the job in a weekend, don't attempt it. Even if you are an old hand at working around the house, you can get bogged down in a large project and lose interest and enthusiasm—and that's when the fun's over and the trouble starts.

Yes, we speak from experience. The only reason we managed to plug along house after house is because of our humble beginnings. The first things we did were cosmetic changes like painting a cabinet or refinishing a piece of furniture. We were fortunate enough to begin with projects that we could complete in a few days—things like adding shelves in the attic for storage or building an attractive little piece of furniture.

Consider this book of fifty-two projects (one for every weekend of the year) a primer, a beginner's workbook to get you started. Even if you are experienced, there is something here for you. No matter which projects you choose you'll save money doing them yourself and enjoy a wonderful feeling of self-fulfillment when you've completed them. By tackling doable projects now, you'll acquire the skills, tools, and confidence you'll need to see you through more complex improvements in the future.

If you're like most of us, you don't have a fancy workshop equipped with expensive tools at home. And that's okay because you don't need them. The projects in this book range from sewing to woodworking; all are easy to complete and require limited space and tools. The woodworking projects use dimensional lumber available at all lumberyards and home centers. None of the projects require ripping wood (cutting lengthwise) so a handsaw and a few other tools (which are specified) are all that's required. Throughout the book we suggest tips and tricks for each project that will guarantee results that will make you proud.

Our instructions give you confidence to tackle and complete the job because we prepare you in the "Getting Ready" section and specify everything that you need in the "Materials, Supplies, Tools" listing. The step-by-step instructions in "Here's How" explain in words and clear illustrations exactly how to do it.

We hope that you'll find the perfect project to get you started, and we guarantee you'll feel a sense of satisfaction when you receive your first compliment on it and can say, "Thanks, I did it myself."

CHAPTER ONE

The Finishing Touch: Painting and Finishing

Faux or Fantasy Finishes

A decorative paint finishing technique can do a lot to jazz up a dull wall or add some pizzazz to a plain piece of furniture. Using four basic techniques, we'll show you how to create one-of-a-kind effects that are limited only by your imagination.

If you can crumple up wads of paper, you can master stippling and dragging. These two easy techniques allow you to create a textured finish on just about any surface. If you have done any painting before, you probably already have splattered some paint around; we'll just show you how to splatter creatively. With this technique you can quickly make interesting finishes that can have a granitelike look. Combing is another easy-to-master technique that uses a homemade cardboard comb to create an interesting striped or streaked effect.

You can use these techniques on walls, furniture, floors, or ceilings. Any surface that can be painted can have a faux finish. Most of the time you will get the best results if a new base coat of paint is applied before any of these techniques are used. This new coat of paint becomes the canvas or background for a new finish.

GETTING READY

Preparing the surface for your faux finish isn't hard; in fact, if the surface is painted and in good condition, a faux finish can be applied directly to it. If the color is right, you need only to make sure that the surface is clean and free of dust and grease. If the paint is dirty, wash it down with a mild soap (such as trisodium phosphate, TSP) and water. If it's clean, just vacuum up any dust and wash or wipe down the wood moldings and trim.

Repaint the room if the paint is dingy or the wrong color, or if the walls are cracked. A basic paint job isn't difficult and it creates a fresh palette for your artwork. Before repainting patch any hairline cracks or holes with a spackling compound, and when it's dry sand it smooth. Use a 2-inch brush to outline the room where the ceiling meets the walls, at all the corners of the room, and along the baseboard and window and door trim. Then use a paint roller to roll out even layers of paint on the walls.

When choosing paints use acrylic or latex paints for both the base coat and decorative finishes. These water-based paints are easy to use because they dry quickly and clean up easily with water. For some of these finishes you'll want to water down the paint to make it thinner and easier to apply.

If you are going to apply a faux finish to a piece of furniture, the same basic idea applies. If the finish is in good shape and the right color, apply the decorative finish directly over it.

If not, sand the piece so that it is smooth and then apply the new base coat. If the surface was previously painted, just sand it so that the existing paint loses its shine and all the areas are uniformly smooth to the touch. If the furniture is unfinished, it should be sanded smooth and then given a coat of primer paint to seal its surface. After the primer has dried, give it a light sanding and apply the base coat of paint.

HERE'S HOW

For any of these finishes it's a good idea to experiment at first on old newspaper to see the different effects you can create. When you find the "look" that you want, you're ready to begin.

Stippling and Dragging.   *Stippling* is used effectively on a wall or large surface where you want to diffuse a color, such as softening a deep blue with a lighter, paler shade. *Dragging* one shade of paint over another creates similar effects to stippling, but it's more pronounced and can be very dramatic. When using either technique, work on one wall or surface of a piece of furniture at a time.

Stippling. *Use clear plastic food wrap as an applicator to create a stippled effect on furniture or walls.*

Begin at the top or where the wall joins the ceiling and work your way down to the baseboard. Work across the wall and then down. When one wall is completed, begin another wall. As you proceed stand back and peruse the wall from a distance so you'll see the overall effect you're creating.

To create a *stippled* finish, use wads of plastic food wrap to apply the final finish glaze coat of paint. Crumple the plastic wrap up to make a "rag" or "applicator." Dip it into a tray of paint and then dab it gently onto newspaper to release some of the paint. Dab the plastic wrap coated with paint on the base coat. As you work turn the pad slightly to vary the pattern.

When the plastic wrap becomes so saturated with paint that it's a blob of paint without any pattern, it's time to replace it with a new wad. You don't want an abrupt change in the pattern, so when you see the pattern diminishing leave some areas where you're working empty. Then feather in the old and new patterns by filling in those empty spaces with the new wad. Continue dabbing the paint on the wall and replacing the plastic wrap as needed until the wall is completed. Then begin at the top of the adjoining wall and work your way around the room.

Use a smaller wad of plastic wrap to dab paint into corner areas. A narrow wad about six inches long makes dabbing paint around window and door trim easier.

Dragging one shade of paint over another creates an interesting tone-on-tone pattern. You can use just about anything to drag the glaze over the surface. We like using a 5½- to 6-inch-wide wallpaper paste brush as an applicator because it produces an interesting striped pattern. This custom finish tends to look somewhat like corduroy fab-

Dragging. *To add subtle shading of colors to a wall, drag a lighter-colored shade of paint across a wall with a wallpaper paste brush.*

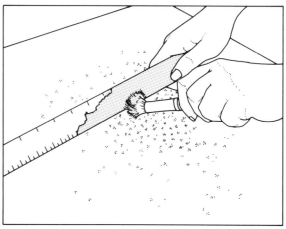

Splattering. *A metal ruler and a stencil brush team up to create a textured look called splattering that uses several different colors of paint.*

ric, with an appealing, two-dimensional texture.

To create this effect, dip the brush into the paint and then release the excess paint by dabbing the brush onto newspaper. Practice on the newspaper before you tackle the wall. Try to drag the brush quickly down the newspaper. If you vary the speed and pressure, you get different effects. Experiment until you find how much paint you need in the brush, how fast to move it, and how hard to press to get the look you want.

After some practice, begin at the top of the wall at the ceiling and drag the brush down the wall. You'll have to do this several times to apply paint from the top to the bottom of a wall. The trick to getting an unbroken swipe of paint on the wall is to avoid stopping or lifting the brush abruptly. Just before you complete the swipe, lift the brush gently so it doesn't leave a deep impression of paint where you lift it off the wall.

About two feet before reaching the baseboard, switch your brush from going down to going up. Begin the swipe of paint at the baseboard and

move it up to meet the upper edge of paint. As you begin your next row at the top of the wall, take care not to end and start new applications directly next to those painted in your first row. Stagger where you begin and stop the brush so there's no definite line that runs across the wall.

Splattering. This technique creates a contemporary look and is perfect for furniture surfaces. For example, used as a tabletop treatment, splattered paint gives a rugged, textured look. Used to paint a flower pot or planter, it can look like granite or stone. You need at least three different paint colors and a metal ruler to splatter the paint from a stencil brush. While it's one of the simplest forms of decorative painting, splattering takes time. You should wait for each splattering to dry before applying another one.

Practice the technique on newspaper to get the hang of it. This can be messy because you're bound to get paint on your hands. Wearing rubber gloves will prevent this. Hold the ruler in one

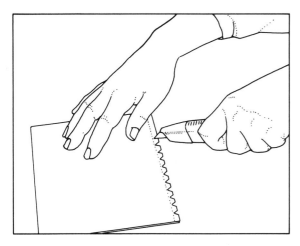

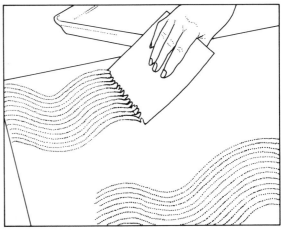

Combing. *To make your own comb, use a square of cardboard and measure off ¼-inch increments. Then cut out the space between them to make a comb.*

Apply a coat of paint to the base paint and then comb through it. Hold the comb firmly and apply even pressure to its entire width.

hand at an angle to the surface being painted and dip the brush into the first color of paint that you're using. Dab off any dripping paint but keep the brush filled with paint. Firmly hold the brush against the ruler and push the brush *away from it.* This technique "spanks" the paint onto the surface with a wide spray of splatters.

Cover the surface with the first color thoroughly and uniformly so there's a natural spray of color across it. Occasionally wipe off excess paint from the ruler. When the paint has dried, continue the process with at least two more applications of different colors of paint.

Combing. This technique is suitable for any painted surface, such as the walls of a room or as a decorative outline on a china cabinet. You paint the surface with a brush and then comb a design through it. Make your own comb using a piece of cardboard cut to the width of your design. We used a 7-inch-square piece with teeth cut out every ¼ inch. Mark off the increments on one

edge of the cardboard. Then use a utility knife to cut it out, working on a workbench or a piece of scrap lumber to protect the surface below it.

Practice the technique on newspaper by experimenting with your comb. For a more intricate pattern, use several different sizes of combs to create a special design.

Begin by laying on the paint with a brush in an area about a foot wide. Then beginning at the top of a wall or at one end of a piece of furniture, hold the comb firmly and drag it through the wet paint. To make certain the design pattern comes out, apply pressure evenly to the comb. When you've combed through the wet paint and completed one pass, wipe off any excess paint on the comb. Continue combing the surface and then let it dry thoroughly.

To provide top coat protection to any painted furniture, it's a good idea to apply a coat of polyurethane. This, as with all painting, is best done in an area with good lighting, which will help you avoid drip and brush marks.

5

Project 2

Paint a Piece of Furniture

Colorful furniture is an element of many of today's popular design trends. Country furnishings are rich in reds, blues, and greens; contemporary settings use bold primary colors; and the Southwestern look includes shades of teal blue and peach.

To brighten a room with color, begin with the furnishings. Choose a small table, chair, or even a picture frame as your first painting project. A likely candidate is something that is already painted. Another good choice is a piece of inexpensive furniture—made of particle board or pine—that is meant to be painted. Sometimes these pieces are made of mismatched wood and are covered with a dark, heavy stain to conceal imperfections.

If you don't already have something to paint, look around at flea markets or garage sales. You can usually find an inexpensive small table or chair that is suitable for painting.

Once you've practiced a bit on a small piece you're ready to tackle larger furniture. But start small so you can complete the project in a weekend and enjoy it immediately.

GETTING READY

The actual painting is the fun part of this project, but to do the job right you will probably spend more time preparing to paint. If it seems as if we spend a lot of time explaining how to sand and fill, it's because the preparation of the surface separates a professional-looking paint job from a mediocre one.

If your piece of furniture has drawers or removable parts, disassemble it. We used an ordinary screwdriver to remove the upholstered seat top of our bench. Remove any hardware such as decorative drawer pulls, hinges, or other decorations.

When shopping for materials, purchase a good-quality paintbrush. We found that a polyester brush is the best buy. It holds a lot of paint and has thin bristles that lay down a smooth coating. For the most part you get exactly what you pay for. You can't expect a two-dollar paintbrush to perform like a ten-dollar brush. A good brush will not make you a professional painter, but you will find it very hard to get a good finish with a cheap tool.

Be sure to protect the area where you'll work. Lay down a drop cloth or layers of newspapers on the floor or work surface.

Good lighting is also important for both the preparation work and paint application. Place a floor lamp with its shade removed to expose the bare bulb or use a clip-on work lamp so that it shines directly on the side of the furniture that you're working on.

Naturally, since you're painting you should protect yourself by wearing work clothes that a splatter of paint won't harm.

HERE'S HOW

First, survey all surfaces for scratches, dents, and nicks. These areas require filling with a wood filler so the surface is consistently level and smooth. We like using a two-part wood filler system with a hardener and filler that you mix together. Use a small putty knife to mix the two parts and then cover the area being filled with the mixture. Spread it on so it's slightly higher than the surface. Feather out the filler by spreading it onto the surface around the edges. When the filler has dried, sand the patched area with a fine grit abrasive paper. A second application is usually needed for a deep scratch to bring the filler to the level of the surrounding surface. Use filler wherever there's damage to the surface so you have a smooth area to paint.

Sanding the entire surface is the next step to prepare furniture for painting. Use a fine grit abrasive paper and sand all the surfaces uniformly. To sand difficult-to-reach areas like the curved surfaces of table or chair legs, make a sanding belt out of cloth or masking tape and sandpaper. Just stick the tape to the back of the sandpaper and then cut the sandpaper into narrow strips. Work these strips back and forth—sort of like dental floss—to sand in crevices and around legs. After sanding wipe down the piece with a tack rag, which is a piece of sticky cheesecloth made to pick up dust, or a rag dampened with mineral spirits. Now it's ready to be painted.

Use a latex semigloss paint and a polyester brush to apply it. Stir the paint with a stick until it's completely mixed and runs smoothly when you hold the stick up over the can. All the pigments should be mixed so there's one consistent color, with no streaking of shades in the paint. Dip the brush into the paint until the bristles are filled with paint halfway up. Gently tap the brush on the side of the can to prevent it from dripping and hold the brush at an angle as you spread on the paint. If you get too much paint in a corner, press the brush against the side of the can to remove paint and use the brush to pull out the excess paint.

Begin by turning the piece upside down and painting the inside surfaces of the framework. Then move the piece to its upright position and work from the inside out. Move the furniture as you paint so that you're applying paint to a horizontal surface. This will prevent runs and drips and assure you of a good finishing coat. On our stool we painted in this order: the interior of the top section, the bottom cross braces, the four upper side pieces, and the legs.

Work in small areas so you can retain the "wet

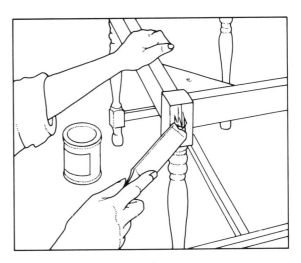

Use a wood filler to fill in holes, crevices, or scratches on the surface. When dry, sand the area smooth.

edge," as painters call it. All that means is that you should not paint a large area or in one direction for so long a time that when you return to painting the adjacent area the paint has started to "set up," or dry. Applying paint over paint that has set up causes lap marks. This varies according to the type of paint you use and the humidity and temperature. You will have to experiment to find how much area you can paint and still keep a wet edge.

If you do get drips or lap marks, let them dry. You will only make things worse if you go back over the area with the brush. Sand the area smooth after the paint is hard and repaint it.

If you're painting both sides of a cabinet door, work on one side at a time, including the edges. When that's completely dry, turn it over so you can paint the opposite side. When all surfaces are painted, take a look at the overall piece. Does it need a second coat of paint? It does if the paint is lighter in some areas than others or if you're cover-ing a dark shade with a lighter one. If the surface has heavily patched or discolored areas, you might want to give it another coat of paint. If so, repeat the process and let it dry thoroughly.

Wash out the brush and paint stick with soap and water and let them dry before storing. Always clean painting tools immediately after use.

Complete the project by installing the piece's hardware (new or original), and then put your furniture in place so you can enjoy using it.

Materials, Supplies, Tools

sandpaper	polyester brush
sanding strips	tack rag or rag dampened
wood filler	with mineral spirits
latex semigloss paint	drop cloths, newspapers
putty knife	

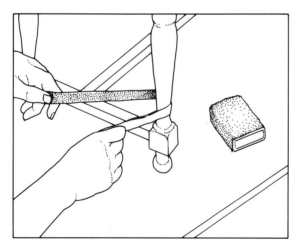

You can buy a flexible sanding block (it's a sponge wrapped in sandpaper) for sanding flat surfaces; for curved areas make your own sanding strips with tape and sandpaper to work the strips back and forth.

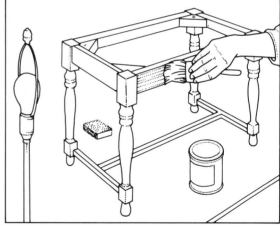

As you paint, make sure you have enough good lighting so you can see what you're doing and prevent drips, runs, and brush marks in the paint.

Project 3

Spray Paint Metal Furniture

Don't think of metal furniture strictly as a glass-topped table and chairs used outdoors on the patio. You'll find metal bed frames are more popular today than ever before. Storage cabinets and utility carts made of metal are used in many kitchens, and metal file cabinets are a mainstay in the home office.

Since most metal objects have a painted finish, it's easy to salvage a piece of metal furniture and give it some pep and pizzazz with a paint job. In just a few hours we transformed an abandoned metal coffee table that was left for garbage pickup by a neighbor. Painting metal is easy, especially since there are spray paints designed especially for the job. Rusted and pitted metal can be repaired and renewed using a two-part filler.

GETTING READY

Getting a metal surface ready for spraying requires careful preparation. Metal is smoother than wood, and not as porous, so any blemishes will stand out in the finish. This is especially true if you use a high-gloss enamel, a finish that exaggerates flaws because it is so reflective.

It is important to take the time to remove rust, chipped paint, scratches, or gouges. By filling in depressed areas with a two-part polyester-based filler, most metal surfaces are easy to repair. Top this new smooth surface off with spray paint and you can achieve an almost flawless finish that

lets the entire piece of furniture look brand new.

Spray painting is messy, so protect the work area with layers of newspaper or with a drop cloth. The overspray can drift way beyond the area being painted, so extend the protection at least three feet out from the piece of furniture. The fumes from spray paint are toxic, so provide plenty of ventilation (work in an open garage or outside, if possible). Otherwise, purchase a respirator mask—not just a dust mask—and wear it during spraying.

HERE'S HOW

Begin by taking apart any movable pieces. If it's a metal card table chair with a removable seat or back cushion, take it apart. See if shelves or cabinet drawers can be removed. Remove rubber caps on the feet of chairs or table legs, the glass from a tabletop, or the head- and footboard of a metal bed.

Where there is unremovable trim, such as drawer pulls on a file cabinet, use masking tape to protect them from paint. If the hinges are welded or pressed permanently in place, leave them alone and mask the hardware, hinges, and anything else that you don't want painted.

What you use to sand the metal surface depends on the depth of the damage. A wire brush with a wooden handle and stiff wire bristles is a good tool for removing flaky paint and rust. You can also purchase an inexpensive circular wire brush attachment for an electric drill to make this part of the project a lot easier. We recommend you purchase one of these attachments if you face a deeply rust-pitted piece of metal or one with several layers of flaking paint. With the circular wire brush you can *feather* (grind smooth) the ridges between the paint layers so they'll become a smooth surface. While doing so, you'll create a shower of loose paint chips and rust dust, so wear eye protection and put down plenty of paper or drop cloths to protect your work area.

After all loose paint and rust areas are wire-brushed, give a complete sanding to all other surfaces. This will "rough them up," producing a good bonding surface for the new paint.

If there are a few minor scratches left or pitted areas caused by rust, fill them with a two-part polyester filler, available in most hardware stores. Prepare the polyester filler according to the manufacturer's directions. Apply it with a putty knife, filling scratches or depressed areas slightly higher than the surface of the metal. When the filler has hardened (usually in about twenty minutes) sand the areas smooth and feather the edges out with a piece of medium grit sandpaper stretched over a sanding block. A foam sanding block (which is a piece of foam encased in sandpaper) works particularly well if the surfaces are curved, since it can bend to the contour of the metal.

When sanding is completed, wipe down the piece of furniture with a rag dampened with mineral spirits.

We chose a gloss enamel spray paint with a built-in primer because it blocks moisture and protects the metal surface from corrosion. Whatever paint you choose, though, use the primer recommended by the manufacturer. The proper primer paint combination is especially important

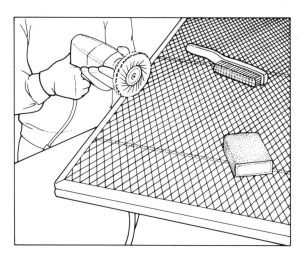

To grind out rusted areas or deep gouges in metal, use a circular wire brush attachment for an electric drill. For minor rust marks or scratches use a sanding block.

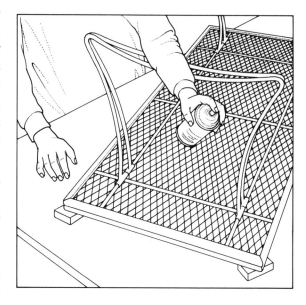

Hold the can of spray paint at a slight angle to the object, directing its nozzle to the surface. Keep the can moving. It's better to give furniture two light coats of spray paint than one heavy application, which can cause runs and drip marks.

when painting metal. Unless the paint system can keep moisture from the metal, it will rust under the paint, causing it to eventually peel.

It is also important that you follow the paint manufacturer's directions and shake the can of paint. *You can't shake it too much.* If anything, you won't shake it enough. Most manufacturers of spray paint recommend that you shake a can for a full minute or at least until you can hear the mixing ball inside rattling around.

You will get a better paint job if you apply at least two light applications of spray paint instead of one heavy coat. The paint comes out of the nozzle in a fine mist. The closer the nozzle is held to the metal, the more paint is deposited on the surface. Hold the can about a foot from whatever you are painting and move the can parallel to the surface. Don't move the can in an arc or you will get uneven coverage at the corners, since the nozzle is farther from the surface at the end of the arc as you swing back and forth. Make a few practice runs on a piece of newspaper until you see that you are laying down an even coat of paint.

Keep the can moving or you will apply too much paint in one area and cause a drip or run. It also helps to try to have all surfaces you are painting horizontal, letting gravity spread the paint instead of causing it to run.

If you do get a drip or run, let it dry. Don't try to smooth the paint out by spraying more—you'll only make it worse. Later when the paint has dried, sand the run marks away and give it a quick touch-up spray. The same solution works for fingerprints or smudges in wet paint. Position the piece of furniture so you can begin spraying its interior, then work on its back or bottom next. Turn the piece. You might have to wait until the paint is dry before turning it. Paint all of its outer surfaces and then its top or front panels. When you have to turn over or reposition the furniture, do it carefully.

Materials, Supplies, Tools

drop cloths, newspapers
masking tape
wire brush or electric drill with circular wire brush attachment
foam sanding block
two-part polyester-based filler
mineral spirits
rags
spray paint for metal with built-in primer
respirator mask

Source

Derusto (rust preventive enamel) by DAP, Inc. Dayton, OH 45401

Project 4

Dye Furniture

While a painted finish on furniture creates a striking splash of color, you can achieve a subtle, softer look using liquid dye as a wood stain. When used on unfinished wood furniture, this age-old technique produces a subdued wash of color that gives any piece an entirely new personality. Applying dye over an already painted piece works nicely, too. You can apply dye over a whitewash base coat or to wood that has been stripped of old paint.

The key to this process is not the dye itself, but rather the thin whitewash base applied before the dye. This step—sometimes called "pickling" —gives the dye a consistent, nonporous base and prevents a blotchy and uneven finish.

To protect the new finish that we applied to our storage bench, we gave it a top coat of polyurethane so it could withstand the bumps and nicks of use and abuse.

GETTING READY

If the piece of furniture has many parts, disassemble it. Remove drawers and hardware and set them up in a work area that has good lighting and floor protection. Use old bed sheets or blankets or layers of newspapers over a plastic drop cloth, which can be an old shower curtain liner. Protect yourself by wearing old clothes. Raise the piece of furniture by placing it on scrap lumber or bricks,

anything that will lift it up a few inches. This makes it easier to paint the lower surfaces without moving and turning it.

Staining with dye works best on bare wood, whether new or old. We used a liquid dye straight out of the bottle on unfinished wood. To remove a finish such as varnish, polyurethane, resin, or wax from an old piece, use a paint stripper (see pages 15–17). The piece should have no color in it for best results. Let it dry thoroughly before sanding.

A good sanding is the next step after stripping off the old finish to smooth the unfinished wood. Use a medium grit #120 sandpaper and go over all areas so the surface is sanded consistently. Then use a tack rag or a rag dampened in mineral spirits to remove grit or dust from the sanding.

HERE'S HOW

The fun part of this project is watching the color make the wood come to life. The first step is applying a whitewashing undercoat to all surfaces. We found that white flat latex paint works well for this process—it's also inexpensive and dries fast. Use a 3-inch-wide foam brush to apply it to the wood, then wipe the paint off with a clean rag before the paint has a chance to get tacky. (This will get messy, so wear rubber gloves and work in a small area.) You want to remove most of

Use a foam brush to spread liquid dye straight from the bottle onto the dry whitewashed surface. Apply the dye going with the grain of the wood, working it into crevices, corners, and grooves.

the brush into the dye and paint it on the white-washed surface. Use a rag to wipe off the excess dye. Turn the rag frequently and use and reuse it until it's filled with dye. As you pull away the excess dye, you'll see how the color blends into the surface, revealing soft, subtle tones. Here again, if you want a darker shade, use a second application of dye after the first has dried. If you leave too much dye on the first time around, you can't lighten the finish later.

For tight corners and crevices use a cotton swab to both wipe on the dye and wipe it off. If there's a long continuous groove (like on our storage chest) use the blade of a spatula covered with a rag to wedge the dye into this kind of difficult-to-

the paint so that what little does remain on the wood appears as a translucent film.

You can create different effects by the amount of paint you leave on the wood surface; the more paint you remove, the more the wood grain will show through. Likewise, if you leave too much paint on the surface, the grain of the wood will be hidden. We found that it's better to wipe most of the paint off, and then, if you want to hide more of the grain, apply a second coat. When the entire surface is whitewashed let it dry thoroughly.

Pour the liquid dye straight out of the bottle into a plastic container and put on rubber gloves. Work on a small section (approximately two feet by two feet) at a time to complete the process. Dip

With a clean rag, wipe the excess dye off the surface. Gently swab up the dye, working in the direction of the wood grain.

reach area. Use the same trick with a clean rag to pull excess dye *out* of a tight space.

Let the dye dry and see if the color appeals to you. If you want it deeper or darker, then repeat the dyeing process.

When you've achieved the color you want, take the final step of providing tough top coat protection with polyurethane. Use a bristle brush and an alkyd-based polyurethane for best results.

Source

Rit Liquid Dye, CPC, International Inc.
P. O. Box 21070
Indianapolis, IN 46221

Materials, Supplies, Tools

liquid dye	medium grit sandpaper
plastic container	drop cloths
foam brush	off-white flat latex paint
rubber gloves	several clean rags
tack rag	

Project 5

Refinish a Piece of Wood Furniture

Do you have a hidden treasure buried down in the basement or tucked away in the attic? Don't think so? Take another look—you might find an old piece of furniture that's ripe for refinishing. If you don't, head for a flea market or yard sale. That's where we found a small side table with spindle legs and a handy bottom shelf.

A small and manageable chair, footstool, or table is an ideal first-time project for a weekend refinisher. You don't need a workshop to refinish a small piece like this—the floor or a tabletop will do just fine. Tackling a small piece almost guarantees good results because you won't get bogged down. You'll complete the job in a weekend and can use and enjoy your instant heirloom right away. The success will encourage you to tackle a larger piece next time.

G E T T I N G   R E A D Y

Before the weekend, test the finish on the furniture that you plan to refinish (see box on page 16). This simple test tells you whether to purchase a paint remover or furniture refinisher. You can then do your shopping for supplies and gather together all the materials so you'll be ready to start.

It doesn't matter whether you need to use a paint remover or furniture refinisher because both of these products are applied in the same way. The main difference is that furniture refinisher melts off a lacquer finish almost instantly, while it takes at least ten minutes for paint remover to loosen a thick coat of paint or a heavy layer of varnish. Before you use either product, carefully read and follow the manufacturer's directions provided on the can.

Give some thought to choosing a work area. It must have good ventilation and be safe from inquisitive little ones. (Refinishing is a messy job involving caustic chemicals, so you don't want the kids playing nearby.) Good lighting is important, so bring in additional lamps or a work light if there's not adequate lighting.

H E R E ' S   H O W

Before you start any refinishing project, protect the surrounding area. The easiest way to do this is to lay down a thick plastic drop cloth or several plastic garbage bags with their edges overlapped on the work surface. It may be the floor, a tabletop, or plywood on workhorses; whatever it is, protect it from the chemicals you'll be using. On top of the plastic spread several layers of newspapers. Place your piece of furniture on the newspaper with an aluminum pan under each of its legs to catch the drips.

Steel wool is packaged in rolls that should be unfolded before using. Unfold each piece and cut or tear it in half to make a wadded-up pad. Then gather all the remaining supplies and materials together and carefully reread the directions of the paint remover or furniture refinisher you're using.

Since our table had a varnish finish, we used a paint remover to strip the piece for refinishing.

Put on rubber gloves and pour paint remover into an aluminum or glass container. Brush on the remover with a bristle brush, applying it evenly and in the direction of the grain of the wood (if you can see it). Almost immediately you'll see the chemicals go to work, but don't rush the process. Wait until the finish bubbles up and pulls away from the wood surface before you try to remove it. When the finish is loose, remove the old finish with a wad of steel wool. The steel wool acts like a mop as the fine wire pad cuts away any stubborn finish that might remain. Turn the steel wool pads frequently so you have a clean side working on the finish. And use lots of them.

If there's only one coat of finish, your job will be easy. If there's more than one layer of finish on the piece, the job becomes more time-consuming, since several applications of remover are needed.

When you apply remover to curved surfaces such as spindle legs, brush it on, making sure you cover all the areas. You will find it helps to turn the piece upside down or on its side to get at difficult-to-reach areas.

When all the finish is removed, wipe down the piece with a rag soaked in mineral spirits to remove any leftover finish that you missed. Let the piece dry thoroughly for a few hours. Then give it a light sanding with #220 grit abrasive paper. Wipe the sawdust off the wood with a tack rag, which is a piece of sticky cheesecloth made to pick up fine dust.

Now you're ready for the fun part. We used a paste stain and varnish because these rub-on finishes are so easy to use. All you have to do is wipe the stain on with a clean rag, making sure that you coat the surface evenly. Then let it dry overnight. Complete the job with a paste varnish finish to provide top coat protection.

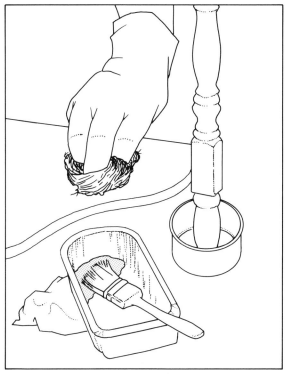

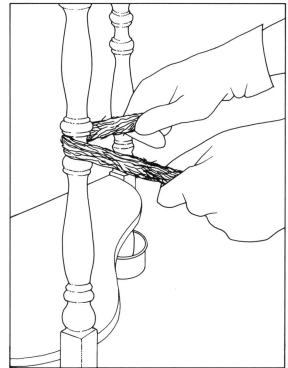

Use plenty of steel wool to mop up the old finish and remover. If some of the finish remains, apply more remover to the area and then remove with steel wool.

To get old finish out of tight crevices, use a church key–type can opener or a cotton swab dipped in the remover. For chair and table leg spindles use a strip of steel wool or string (the same diameter as the groove) dipped in remover. Work the steel wool strip or string back and forth around the spindle as if you were using dental floss.

Materials, Supplies, Tools

heavyweight rubber
  gloves
drop cloths: newspapers
  and plastic sheeting,
  drop cloth, or garbage
  bags
paint stripper or furni-
  ture refinisher
medium and fine grade
  steel wool
church key–type can
  opener

string
old bristle paintbrush
aluminum pans or
  glass containers
mineral spirits
sanding block
tack rag
paste finishes: stain,
  varnish
plenty of clean rags

Source

Bartley Gel Finishes
  29060 Airpark Dr.
  Easton, MD 21601

Project 6

Stencil-Paint a Floor Cloth

Before there were manufactured floor coverings such as linoleum, creative homeowners painted their own decorative floor cloths. Not only did these canvas floor coverings add color and decoration to a room, they also helped keep out cold drafts from the uninsulated floors of long ago.

Using an ordinary artist's canvas and some acrylic paints, you can create your own floor cloth—perhaps not to combat the cold, but as a decorative addition to your home. You can paint your own design freehand or use a stencil design. For a fanciful look, we used as a stencil a piece of an old lace curtain that we found at a rummage sale. You can even use an old doily or dresser scarf to create a pattern that pleases you.

We covered a 24-by-36-inch canvas with dark green acrylic paint and let it dry. Then we centered and laid the lace curtain on the canvas. We used spray adhesive to keep the lace stencil in place while we sprayed the canvas with cream-colored water-soluble paint. When it dried we peeled off the lace curtain to reveal the pattern.

GETTING READY

Protect the work area with layers of newspaper. Position the canvas on top of the newspaper in such a way that you can move around it. Provide yourself with plenty of ventilation while you are spraying. If you can't work outside or in an open garage, wear a respirator mask to protect yourself from the paint fumes.

We found that an artist's canvas that is already stretched and stapled to a frame is easiest to work on. The frame keeps the canvas flat while you work; after it's painted you can remove the staples from the frame to release the canvas.

HERE'S HOW

Use a 3-inch or wider paintbrush to apply a base coat of acrylic paint. Acrylic paint comes in a tube and is too thick to brush directly on the canvas. Thin the paint by squeezing some into a food tray or another shallow container and then add water. Dilute the paint just enough so it flows freely onto the canvas. Brush on the paint in an even pattern so that the base coat is consistent and evenly applied.

When the base coat is dry, align the lace curtain or whatever you plan to use as a stencil so the pattern is positioned to your liking. Move it around until you're satisfied with how the pattern lines up on all four sides. When you're satisfied with the layout, lift one side of the stencil, folding it back on itself. Spray the exposed area of the canvas with spray adhesive and replace the lace stencil, smoothing it in place. Then repeat this process on the other side to secure the entire stencil to the canvas. Use pushpins in the sides of

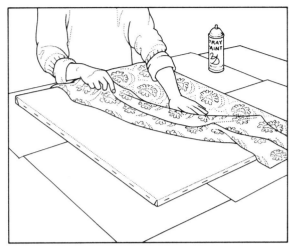

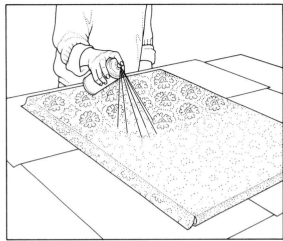

Align the lace stencil (curtain) carefully on the canvas so the pattern is spaced evenly on all four sides. Use spray adhesive to secure it in place and pushpins in the sides of the wooden frame to hold it taut.

Evenly spray water-soluble paint onto the lace stencil, beginning at one side and working your way from one end to the other. Move around the canvas as you spray so the paint is applied evenly on all surfaces.

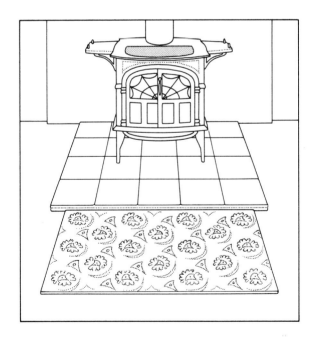

A final coat of spray polyurethane gives the finished floor cloth added protection.

the frame to secure the sides of the stencil to the four sides of the frame.

Shake a can of flat water-soluble paint until the ball inside it rattles, telling you it's ready to use. Begin spraying at one side of the canvas, moving the can in a steady motion parallel to the canvas. Move around the canvas as you spray and keep the can the same distance from the canvas throughout the application. This guarantees that an even coat of paint is applied to all areas of the surface. Try to spray from different angles so the paint works its way completely through the stencil, assuring more complete coverage.

Let the paint dry and then remove the push-pins from the frame. Then carefully peel off the stencil. Protect the canvas with a coat of spray polyurethane. When the top coat is dry, use a screwdriver or small pry bar to remove the staples holding the canvas to its frame.

Fold the unpainted edges of the canvas underneath and glue them down with an all-purpose glue. Carefully flatten the sides and press in place while the glue dries. Then precisely cut at a 45-degree angle through both layers of overlapping fabric at each corner to form a miter. Work slowly so you cut through only the two layers of folded fabric and not through the face fabric. Remove the cutoff pieces and press the adjoining pieces flat.

Materials, Supplies, Tools

newspaper drop cloth
24-by-36-inch artist's canvas
3-inch-wide paintbrush
piece of lace curtain to cover canvas
spray adhesive
acrylic paint
spray flat water-soluble paint
spray polyurethane
all-purpose glue
screwdriver or pry bar

Sources

"Country Treasures" cream satin finish
    DAP, Inc.
    Dayton, OH 45401
"Aleene's Tacky Glue," Artis Inc.
    Solvang, CA 93463

CHAPTER TWO

Home Furnishings for Now and Forever

Project 7

Shortcuts for Ready-to-Assemble Furniture

Today some furniture manufacturers sell "assemble-it-yourself" furniture in boxes complete with all the parts you need to put it together. Since you supply the labor of assembling and finishing, it can be an inexpensive way to furnish or decorate a room.

We're not talking here about high-end unfinished oak furniture or antique replica kits that can be as pricey as finished furniture. We're referring to the less expensive variety of ready-to-assemble furniture that you see advertised at Conran's, Ikea, and other discount chain stores. It's usually constructed of pine or soft wood and created in simple straight knock-down designs for bookcases, chests of drawers, or small desks.

Assembling and finishing this kind of furniture is an ideal weekend project, especially if you plan to try your hand at woodworking but haven't accumulated a workshop full of tools yet. We bought a pine storage chest that's ideal for hiding kid's toys or bed linen that cost only thirty-five dollars. It came all boxed up with precut pieces and the glue, screws, and hardware needed to put it together.

Assembly of these kits is pretty straightforward, but the ones we've used provide minimal information you need to put it together and can often be confusing. Because of this we'd like to expand on the directions. Since we have years of experience building furniture from scratch we've picked up a few tricks that will help you with your first adventure in putting furniture together. Use our advice as a general overall plan and follow the particular assembly directions provided with your kit.

GETTING READY

Assembling furniture takes up lots of room. You need an area where you can lay all the parts out and a large flat table or bench where you can assemble the piece. If you don't have a garage, basement, or workshop, try the kitchen table. We used the kitchen counter for our last project because the room has good lighting—another important feature you'll need.

You'll find small hardware parts for the furniture usually packaged in plastic bags. We think a good way to keep the hardware organized is by separating the various sizes of nails, screws, and hinges in a muffin tin. Lay out and identify all the wooden components or parts of the piece of furniture, and as you're unpacking them try to associate each piece with the assembly diagram and/or the instructions.

HERE'S HOW

Here are some pointers to help you assemble knock-down furniture:

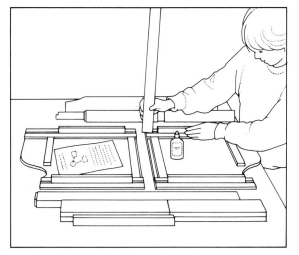

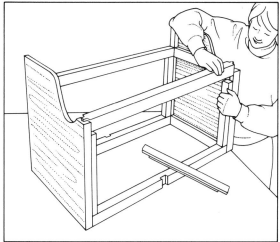

Positively identify each part before assembly. Each part should fit into its slot or groove snugly, but don't force the fit. Apply glue to both mating surfaces.

Place the frame on a flat surface when the glue is drying so the unit will dry straight and square.

- Sand as many of the visible furniture parts and components as you can before you assemble the unit. Be careful not to sand them so much that it changes their shape, especially the end pieces. By sanding the individual parts before assembly you won't be faced with sanding in corners and under hard-to-reach areas that are created as the unit goes together.

- Most furniture kit parts are cut to fit fairly precisely. Unless you are absolutely certain that you are fitting the right part in place, don't force a part into position. If something doesn't fit check to see that you are inserting the part in the correct manner. It might not fit because it's flipped end for end. Also check that you're working with the correct part. If you do have to force a part into place, do it slowly and evenly. Don't hit the part with a

hammer or you will dent it. Place a block of scrap wood against the part and hit the scrap instead.

- Don't spare the glue when you're applying it. You might have to purchase additional glue if there's only a small bottle included in the kit. Before you apply it, make sure which surface should get glue. Apply glue to both mating surfaces and spread it out before you push the parts together. Try to visualize how the part will go in place and how you can best avoid getting glue on visible surfaces. By thinking it through before gluing you can decide if it's better to put the glue on the end of the part or into the groove or in both places.

- Most of the joints are formed by slipping a part into a groove. These can be held together with nails until the glue dries. It is not easy to draw these joints tight using only nails, so purchase a couple of 3-inch C clamps. Use them to hold a stubborn joint tight until the glue sets up. By using clamps you'll be assured of a much stronger joint and will have less cracks to fill when you finish the piece of furniture.

- Whenever you set the unit aside to wait for the glue to dry, make sure that it is sitting on a flat surface. Most of the frames are slightly flexible before the glue dries, and if you set them on an uneven surface they will set up crooked. When the glue dries that's how it will remain. Use a rafter or combination square to check the frame often to make sure everything is in alignment.

- If you do get glue on a visible surface, don't wipe it up—allow it to harden. When it's rubbery or hard, carefully chip the glue off the wood with a sharp chisel. The blade of a screwdriver will work in a pinch but don't gouge the wood with it.

- Glue acts as a sealer on the wood. If you don't completely remove it, the stain or finish can't soak into the wood and you will have a light spot where the glue is. *Be sure to remove all traces of glue before finishing the wood.* To check that the surface of the wood is free of glue, wipe a rag dampened in mineral spirits across it. If the area is not blotchy, the glue is gone and the wood is ready for finishing.

Materials, Supplies, Tools

rafter's or combination square
sandpaper
glue
3-inch C clamps
hammer
screwdriver

Project 8

Reupholster a Dining Room Chair

Even when you include the time it takes to shop for the fabric, changing the upholstery on dining room chairs is one of the quickest ways to spruce up a room. And it's one of the least expensive decorating projects that we know of. For twenty-two dollars we found fabric to recover the backs and seats of four well-worn Scandinavian-style dining room chairs. A rich navy blue wool blend fabric on the chairs transformed our dining room in just one afternoon. Making a tube of fabric to fit snugly over the chair back was all the sewing that was required. To cover the chair seat we used a heavy-duty stapler to secure the new material.

Most fabric-covered seats can be removed by turning the chair over and removing the screws or bolts that hold the seat in place. Our chairs were bought "knocked down"—sometimes known as K-D—which means they were designed to be packaged flat in a box and then easily assembled. An Allen wrench is needed to remove the parts on most of this type of furniture.

Our chairs have removable fabric-covered backs with the fabric stapled in place. The two wooden sides of the frame are attached to the fabric-backed piece by hardware that conceals the staples.

Many traditional dining room chairs have a back made of solid or scrolled wood that makes replacing the seat fabric the only work required.

GETTING READY

Take one of the old seats to a fabric outlet to show the salesperson what you want to cover. If there is padding in good condition beneath the fabric, you can simply recover it. If, however, there is matted-down padding, buy one inch or less foam seat padding to replace it.

For a ballpark estimate of how much fabric is needed for one chair, measure the seat and add four inches to the width and length. This excess material folds over the sides and is stapled in place. Take advantage of the experts at the fabric store where you shop and ask for suggestions about laying out the seat covers on the fabric so you don't buy too much material. For example, if you have a solid or checkered fabric, the cover can be laid out either vertically or horizontally on the material. If you have a stripe or pattern, you're restricted to laying out the seat covers vertically or in such a way that the pattern is centered properly on each seat.

Before you begin, use a steam iron to remove any creases in the fabric and cut away any loose threads from the cut ends.

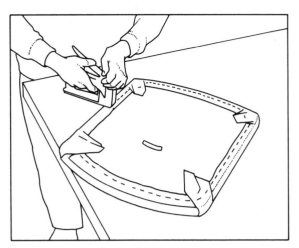

On the chair seat staple one side down and then pull the opposite side taut. Check for wrinkles before you secure the fabric with the stapler. Fold the corners flat and then staple down.

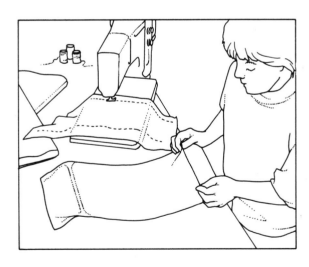

To cover a chair back with a fabric tube, gently pull it over the old cover. Make sure that the tube fits snugly to prevent the fabric from sagging and puckering.

HERE'S HOW

If you're replacing the chair padding, cut it to fit the shape of the seat and use household glue to attach it. Gluing the padding in place isn't always necessary, but if you use a slippery fabric the glue helps hold the padding in place and prevents it from bunching up or moving around while you're stapling the new fabric in place.

Place the fabric right side down on a flat surface. Lay out the old chair seat (square, rectangle, circle, or whatever) facedown on the backside of the fabric. Make sure the pattern is centered and allow for an four-inch overlap on all sides. You can cut out the shape freehand, or if you're not sure-handed, outline the shape on the fabric with chalk.

With the fabric right side down, place the chair seat on it. Recheck pattern alignment and then pull up opposite sides and fold them over on the seat back. Use three staples about two inches apart to hold one of these sides down. Then pull the other side tight and staple it in place. Work on opposite sides and smooth out the fabric on the front of the seat so there is no pulled or tucked fabric. When you get to the corners, pull the fabric up tight and then spread the bunched fabric out and staple it flat.

To cover the back of our chairs we made a fabric tube and pulled it over the back. Make the tube fit snugly so you have to coax it on. If the old covering can be easily removed, take it off and use it as a pattern to make the new one. If not, measure the back with a cloth tape. Measure the circumference of the back then add $1\frac{1}{2}$ inches (for a $\frac{3}{4}$-inch seam) to this figure. Measure the length of the back and add about two inches to allow for one inch at each side for stapling.

If the wood frame of the furniture needs a facelift, it's a good time to give it one while it's completely disassembled. Clean and polish with a wood furniture cleaner and give it a coat of wax for protection. If the finish is paint or polyurethane, sponge wash it with a mild soap and warm water and buff it dry.

Sewing the back cover tube is easy. Fold the fabric right sides together lengthwise. Sew a double running stitch $3/4$ inch from the edge. Trim off the excess fabric.

Turn the tube right side out and coax it onto the back. Pull it onto the back frame, working it as if it were a tight fitting pillowcase on a pillow. If there's a pattern center it on the back, position the tubing so the seam is running straight along the bottom of it. Smooth the fabric across the back.

Staple the ends of the tube to the frame. If the fabric is bulky, you'll have to cut away excess fabric so there's not a double layer. Then reassemble the chair using the hardware you removed.

Materials, Supplies, Tools

sewing machine
fabric to re-cover seats and backs of chairs
padding
measuring tape
household glue (if needed)
heavy-duty stapler
staples
scissors
Allen wrench
screwdriver (if needed)

Project 9

Build a Simple Pine Bench

The versatility of this little bench is only one reason it's one of our favorite projects in this book. You can use it as a coffee table in the den or as a resting place in the hall. Put it under a window or out on the back porch and it becomes a handy plant rest. The straight lines of the bench complement most any style of furnishing, so it's at home in a contemporary setting or a rough-hewn log house. Not only is it attractive, the bench is very easy to build. You can complete the project from start to finish in only a weekend because it has only five parts, each of them cut from readily available dimensional lumber.

G E T T I N G   R E A D Y

When you visit the lumberyard to select the wood for this bench, you might be surprised to learn that clear pine is expensive. You can save money by carefully picking your material from #2 or better pine stock, instead of the higher priced clear pine. Just make sure that the wood is free, or almost free, of knots.

Since the parts are not long (none are over two feet long) another way to economize is to buy scrap pieces of lumber or cutoff pieces. Use the parts list as a guide to find scraps at least two inches longer than required so you can square cut the ends so they look good. You might also find a six- or eight-foot board that has knots and defects,

but has two-foot knot-free sections that you can cut the bench parts from.

The bench is designed so that you can use hand tools and don't have to make any long rip cuts, or lengthwise cuts. The cutouts for the legs and skirt pieces can be made with a coping saw and the other parts can be cut off with a handsaw.

H E R E ' S   H O W

Begin construction by cutting the top and legs to length from the 1 × 12 pine stock. Then cut the skirts from 1 × 4 pine stock. A trick that carpenters use to get a straight square cut is to hold a scrap board along the cut line that guides the saw.

Use a school compass to draw the arch at the bottom of the legs. Set the compass for a $3^1/2$-inch radius and place the point in the center of the leg along the bottom (either of the $11^1/4$-inch sides). Scribe the arch on both leg parts. Set the compass to a $1^1/2$-inch radius and draw the arcs on the bottom edge of the skirts. Place the point of the compass $6^1/4$ inches from the edge. Connect the top of each arch with a line to form the shape of the area that will be cut away from the skirt.

Use a coping or saber saw to cut the arcs from the legs and skirts. Smooth the cut area by sanding them with #120 grit sandpaper. Cut the sandpaper sheet in half and wrap it around a soda can to create a curved sanding surface. Then sand the remaining flat parts with a sanding block.

To create an even line of nails and help position them in the top, draw a layout line across the top beginning 2⅜ inches from each end. Then drive five or six evenly spaced #6d finishing nails along this line. Drive these nails just deep enough so that they start to come out the underside. Position the nails on the skirt with another layout line ⅜ inch from its top edge. Drive six to eight evenly spaced nails into the skirt along this line.

Begin assembly of the bench by applying glue to the top edge of each leg. Position the top on a leg with the nails aligned with the center of the

leg. Drive the outer nails in first, then check to see that the parts are aligned. Drive the remaining nails in, being very careful not to mar the top with the hammer. Install the other leg in the same way.

Place the bench on its side on a flat surface. Use a carpenter's square to check that the legs are square with the top before you install the skirts. Apply glue to the edges of the top and down the leg as far as the skirt will cover (3½ inches). Then place a skirt in position flush with the top edge and even with the ends of the top. Drive the end nails in, recheck the squareness of the legs, and then drive the other nails in. Drive a couple of

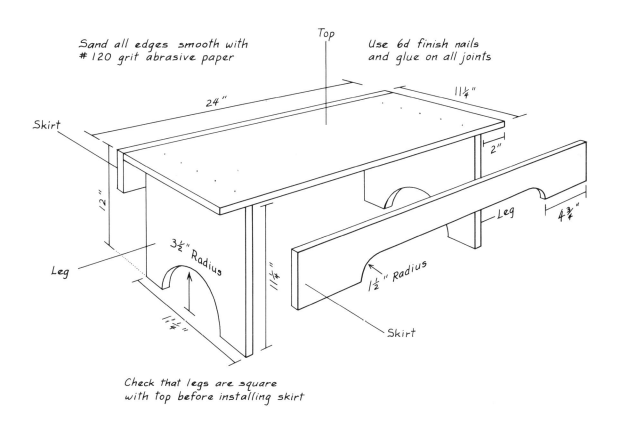

Sand all edges smooth with #120 grit abrasive paper

Top

Use 6d finish nails and glue on all joints

24"

11¼"

Skirt

2"

12"

3½" Radius

11¼"

Leg

4¾"

Leg

1½" Radius

11¼"

Skirt

Check that legs are square with top before installing skirt

PARTS LIST			
NAME	AMOUNT	SIZE	MATERIAL
Top	1	3/4″ × 11½″ × 24″	Pine
Leg	2	3/4″ × 11¼″ × 11¼″	Pine
Skirt	2	3/4″ × 3½″ × 24″	Pine

additional nails through the skirt into the edge of the legs. Install the other skirt on the opposite side in the same way. Go back and countersink each nail head below the surface of the wood with a nailset.

After the glue has dried chip away any excess glue that might have squeezed out of the joints with a wood chisel or screwdriver. Sand the bench—especially the end grain—with #120 grit abrasive paper. Dust off the bench with an old paintbrush or dust brush and then wipe all surfaces with a tack rag (a sticky rag dampened with mineral spirits used to pick up dust).

We used two coats of tung oil, which deepens the color of the wood and brings out the natural grain.

Materials, Supplies, Tools

4½ feet of 1 × 12 pine stock
4½ feet of 1 × 4 pine stock
small bottle carpenter's glue
small box #6d finishing nails
3 sheets #120 grit abrasive paper
sanding block
tack rag, one pint tung oil, clean rags
hammer
nailset
compass
hand or circular saw
coping or saber saw
carpenter's square
paintbrush or dust brush

Project 10

Build and Hang a Bracket Shelf

Dress up this shelf with a treasured porcelain collection in the dining room or dress it down with a stack of colorful cookbooks in the kitchen. Wherever it hangs, this bracket shelf is both attractive and serviceable. Our compact shelf is 7¼ inches deep and 36 inches long, making it ideal for a short hall wall, under a mirror, or in the bathroom to hold toiletries. Two easy-to-make brackets are secured to the wall and then topped with a simple shelf. These three pieces make one attractive unit that can be painted to match any decor.

You have a choice of buying ready-made brackets or making them yourself with the pattern. Ready-made brackets are sold in various styles and sizes in home centers and lumberyards. Choose brackets that are at least six inches deep. Ready-made brackets make this an almost instant project but making them yourself isn't difficult. If you have not done much woodworking, this project is a good way to ease into it.

GETTING READY

When you're making your selection of wood for the shelf, be sure that it is straight and not twisted. The same is true for the material to build the brackets.

Gather the tools, wood, nails, and glue together before you begin construction. You'll need a sturdy work surface where you can cut wood and an area large enough to assemble the shelf unit.

HERE'S HOW

Our instructions begin with making the brackets, so skip ahead if you're using ready-made ones. The first step is enlarging the patterns for the brackets. Draw a grid with one-inch squares on a piece of cardboard. Transfer the shape of the brackets from the small grid pattern to the full-size grid. Make a dot on the small grid every place the outline of the bracket crosses a grid line. Transfer these dots to the corresponding lines on the full-size grid. Then connect the dots to form the pattern.

Copy the pattern as exactly as you can and make the lines connecting the dots smooth so the brackets will have clean, precise lines.

Note that each bracket is made of three parts. The two outer parts are a quarter inch larger than the center bracket. To make certain that the outer parts have the same shape as the center part, make the outer parts first and then use them as the pattern for the inner part pattern.

Align the back edge of the bracket pattern along the edge of the 1 × 6 board and trace the bracket shape on the wood. Use a coping or saber saw to cut the curved sections of the brackets and a hand or circular saw to make the straight cuts.

Sand all cut surfaces smooth. Hold the four outer parts together and sand all edges at the same time to assure that they will have the same shape. Do the same with the two inner parts.

Drive three brads through each outer part

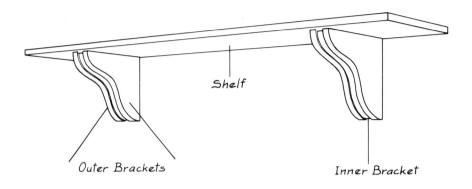

Glue and nail outer brackets
to inner bracket
with 1 inch wire brads

Shelf

Outer Brackets

Inner Bracket

Note :
Attach brackets to wall studs

until the brad point protrudes out of the back. Apply glue to one side of an inner bracket part and then place the outer parts on the inner part. Align these parts along the top and back edges and then nail them together. Turn the unit over and apply glue to the inner part and nail in the outer parts. Assemble the other bracket in the same way.

When the glue is dry, install the two keyhole plates on the back of each bracket to hold it to the wall. Locate the plates on the inner bracket ½ inch down from the top edge and ½ inch up from the bottom edge. Drill a couple of shallow ¼-inch holes behind the screw slot area so there will be room between the plate and wood bracket for the head of the mounting screws.

Cut the shelf to length and sand it smooth.

Also give the brackets a final sanding. Then apply two coats of paint, sanding lightly in between coats.

Secure the brackets to the wall with 2¼-inch #8 round head wood screws driven through the wall into wall studs. Tighten the screws so the heads are about ¼ inch from the wall and then hook the brackets over the screws. If they are loose, tighten the screws a little and the brackets should fit snugly against the wall.

Center the shelf on the brackets and drill a couple of pilot holes for the mounting screws through the top. Keep these holes in the back third of the top. Fasten the top to the brackets with 1¾-inch #8 flat head screws, and the shelf is ready to use.

Inner / Outer Bracket Pattern

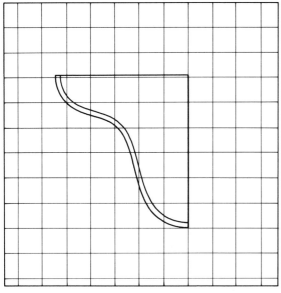

1 square = 1 inch

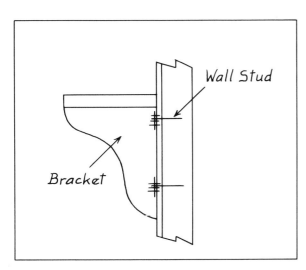

Wall Stud

Bracket

Bracket Mounting Detail

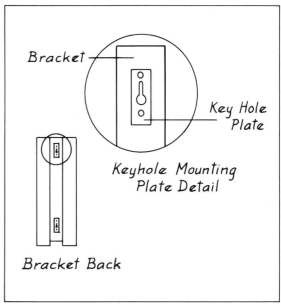

Bracket

Key Hole
Plate

Keyhole Mounting
Plate Detail

Bracket Back

Bracket Back Detail

PARTS LIST

NAME	AMOUNT	SIZE	MATERIAL
Outer bracket	4	$3/4'' \times 6'' \times 5^{1}/_{2}''$	pine
Inner bracket	2	$3/4'' \times 5^{1}/_{4}'' \times 5^{3}/_{4}''$	pine
Shelf	1	$3/4'' \times 7^{1}/_{4}'' \times 36''$	pine
Hanger	4	$1/2''$	metal bracket

Materials, Supplies, Tools

To make a three-foot shelf

4 feet 1 × 8 pine
4 feet 1 × 6 pine
4 steel $1/2$-inch keyhole plates
small bottle of carpenter's glue
small box of $1^{1}/_{4}$-inch wire brads
4 $1^{3}/_{4}$-inch #8 flat head wood screws
2 $2^{1}/_{4}$-inch #8 round head wood screws
3 sheets #120 grit abrasive paper
1 pint paint
paintbrush

hammer
screwdriver
nailset
square
hand or circular saw
coping or saber saw
drill and drill bits
cardboard
pencil

Project 11

Rejuvenate a Director's Chair

A director's chair is versatile, functional, and inexpensive when compared to other furnishings. We've used them just about everywhere inside and outside our house—cozied up to a sofa, at the dining table, and always out on the deck. The four we have on our front porch came from a boat we once owned and had become pretty beaten up by the weather.

The wooden frame of these chairs was in relatively good shape, but the canvas or fabric seat and back covers needed to be replaced. This is an easy project even if you are not an ace sewer. The canvas back cover is nothing more than a straight hemmed panel with wide open pockets at both sides that slip over the back uprights. The chair seats are just wider versions of the back cover but with narrower pockets that hold dowels or battens. This is how these chairs can differ from one another, so take a look at your chair to see how the seat is attached to the frame.

While they're both made of wood, a dowel is round and a batten is square. Usually a dowel or batten fits into a pocket at the end of the seat cover that rests in a slot in the chair frame. The dowel or batten prevents the cover from pulling out of a groove in the frame. In either case all you have to do is duplicate the pocket at the end of the old seat cover and back.

GETTING READY

Collapse the chair and remove the existing back and seat covers. To do this push up the folding hardware on the front and back chair legs. If the hardware is rusted in place, spray on a lubricating oil such as WD-40 so it operates freely.

Check out the dowels to see if they're round or square so you'll make the correct size of pocket for them. Lay down the back and seat covers and measure them. Usually a back measures approximately 5 inches by 21 inches and a seat is about 15 inches by 21 inches.

How you plan to use your chair should determine the type of fabric you pick to replace the covers. If the chair will be used primarily indoors, choose a heavyweight, tightly woven cotton fabric. If it's going to be used outside, you should use a canvas material. Contact a local awning shop where you'll find many synthetic fabrics made especially for outdoor use. This type of fabric resists mildew and discoloration better than traditional canvas.

Whatever fabric you choose, press it smooth with an iron before cutting out the pieces.

HERE'S HOW

The back and seat pieces should be made from double layers of fabric to give them extra strength. Begin by cutting the piece to size. Measure the height of the old back. Double the measurement and add one inch for seam allowance. Measure the length of the old back and add six inches.

To sew the back cover, fold the fabric in half lengthwise, patterned sides together. Stitch the edges together with a $1/2$-inch seam allowance to make a tube. Then cut away the excess material at the seam so it will lie smoothly when pressed. Turn the tube inside out and press the tube flat with the seam at one edge.

Fold each of the two raw side edges over to create an open pocket that slips over the chair back uprights. Fold over each end $2^3/4$ inches and turn the raw edge under about $1/2$ inch. Run this through the machine twice, making a double seam to reinforce it.

To make the seat piece, measure its depth and then double it, adding one inch to the measurement for the seam. Measure how wide it is and add $3/4$ inch to make the dowel or batten pockets. The dimension for these pockets depends on the size of the dowel or batten, so make adjustments accordingly.

Sew the seat into a tube such as you did for the back cover. Make one pocket on either end for the dowel or batten. Place the dowel or batten in the pocket and test its fit in the chair frame. Then sew the second pocket. You should make the new seat so it fits tightly across the frame, allowing the chair frame to fully expand.

Materials, Supplies, Tools

seat and back fabric
thread
sewing machine
scissors
measuring tape
ironing board
iron

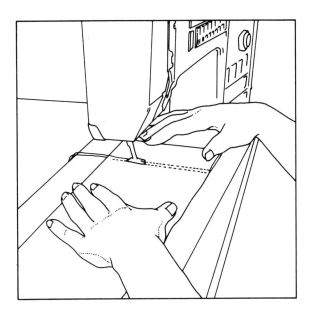

Reinforce the pockets of the back and seat covers by sewing a double stitch. The back should be sized so it is tight between the chair back uprights while allowing the chair to fold out fully.

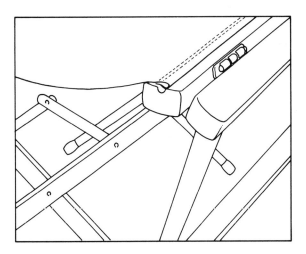

The seat is held in the frame by either a dowel or batten. Check the fit of the first pocket you sew on the new seat cover before you proceed to finish the other side.

Project 12

Skirt a Round Table

If you have a castoff round table that's sturdy—but not too attractive—you can transform it with a colorful skirt. A round table skirted in fabric can be an appealing addition to most rooms because it adds texture and color, not to mention style. You can use a small low table as a nightstand in the bedroom or a wider, higher variety of table as a lamp stand in the den. The skirt provides storage potential, too. The bigger the table, the more you can conceal under its skirt. Whatever its size, a round table skirted in fabric can lend itself to many rooms in a house.

G E T T I N G   R E A D Y

Make it easy on yourself and choose a solid fabric to avoid the hassles of matching patterns at the seams. The tablecloth that we describe fits a standard lamp table that measures 30 inches wide and 29 inches high. To make this we used six yards of 54-inch wide fabric. The wider the fabric you choose, the less sewing you'll have to do.

To determine how much fabric you need, measure the distance from the center of the table to the floor. Add one inch to this figure (for a hem allowance) to find the radius of your circular cover. Double this figure to find the diameter of the skirt and length of the sides of the fabric square you will cut the skirt from. Divide the width of your fabric into this figure and round up to the next whole number. This is the number of panels you need to

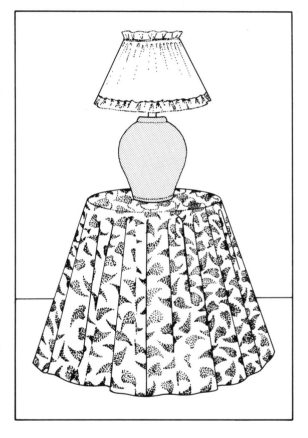

Use six yards of 54-inch-wide fabric to make a skirt for a table as illustrated in the drawing.

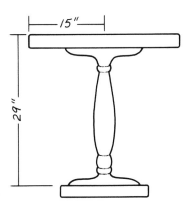

Measure from the center of your table to its edge then from the table edge to the floor. Add these figures together to determine the radius of the skirt.

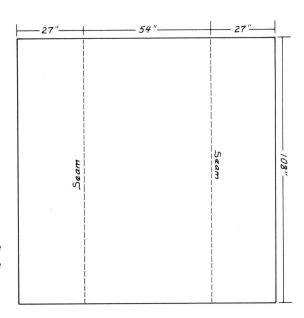

To prevent the seam from running through the middle of the skirt, sew additional 27-inch-wide panels (two halves of the 54-inch-wide fabric) to the sides of the full-width panel.

make the skirt. Multiply the number of panels by their width and you have the size of the fabric square you have to make. Multiply this number by the number of panels to calculate the amount of fabric to purchase. Your answer is in inches so divide it by 36 to get the number of yards needed.

For example, our table measured 15 inches from its center to the edge and 29 inches to the floor. We added a one-inch seam allowance to get a radius of 45 inches. The diameter of the skirt is therefore 90 inches. The fabric is 54 inches wide so two panels are needed to make the square. The fabric square will therefore be 108 inches square, so you have to purchase at least 216 inches (two panels at 108) of fabric or about six yards.

HERE'S HOW

Basically you want to make a square, fold it into quarters, then cut the circle from this fold. Sewing the square is easy but you want to avoid an

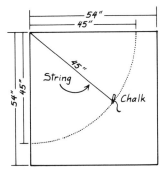

Fold the fabric square into quarters. From the common corner stretch a 45-inch string with chalk tied to it and draw an arc on the fabric. Cut along this line to make the round skirt.

unattractive center seam. So unless your fabric is as wide as the skirt, follow these cutting directions to make the square.

To avoid a center seam we cut one of the 54-inch-wide panels in half to form two 27-inch-wide panels. You only need to do this if your skirt is made from two panels because with three or more panels there is no center seam.

Sew one of the 27-by-108-inch panels to each side of the 54-inch panel to form a square. Open the seams and press them so they lie flat.

Fold the square in half and then in half again so it is one quarter of its original size. Use a piece of chalk tied to a string to help you draw an arc on the fabric. The radius of the skirt is 45 inches, so hold the end of the string at the folded corner of the square. Then pull the chalk and string 45 inches down one edge away from the corner. Hold the string taut at the corner and move the chalk in an arc, tracing it on the fabric.

Trim away the excess fabric below the chalk line. Do this carefully and take your time. If the fabric is too thick to easily cut through, unfold it, continuing the chalk line all around it and cut a single layer of fabric at a time.

Test fit the tablecloth on the table. It will be slightly longer than necessary. Adjust the width of the skirt so there's about 1/2-inch excess for a hem. Then hem the skirt with a clothes iron to press it flat and then run it through the machine.

Materials, Supplies, Tools

approx. 6 yards of 54-inch-wide fabric
thread
sewing machine
scissors
clothes iron
chalk
string

Project 13

Create a Folding Room Screen

A folding screen is a creation you'll find more than one use for. Placed in a corner, it adds height and definition to a room, or used behind a collection of plants, it makes a lovely backdrop. From a practical standpoint, a screen can divide one room into two by defining two separate spaces—such as a study area in a bedroom or a home office in the den.

The primary objective for our design was to make the screen easy to construct. It is composed of three frames that are identical and connected by hinges. These frames are made from dimensional lumber that you can buy at any lumberyard. All you have to do is cut the parts to length from standard 2 × 2 and 2 × 4 pine stock. Using this material prevents you from having to make rip cuts along the length of a board, which is almost impossible to do if you don't have a table saw.

The major parts are joined together with easy-to-make butt joints that are reinforced with flat steel corner braces. The plywood insert panel can be painted, stained, or covered with wallpaper.

GETTING READY

Assemble all your tools, materials, and supplies before you begin. If possible purchase the wood on the weekend before you plan to do this project so it has a chance to dry out during the week. Even though the wood is stored out of the weather in the lumberyard the air conditions in your house are probably drier.

Note that the rail and stile joints are held together with bar clamps while the glue dries. If you don't want to invest in a set of bar clamps use eight-penny finishing nails to hold the parts together while the glue dries.

HERE'S HOW

Each of the three frames is made from two stiles (vertical sides) and two rails (horizontal ends). Begin by cutting the six 72-inch-long stiles from 2 × 2 pine stock. Then cut the six 15-inch-long rails from 2 × 4 pine stock.

You need a large, flat surface to assemble the frames. Lay out the two stiles and two rails to make one frame. Apply carpenter's glue to the ends of the rails. Place the parts in position with the end of each stile so it's flush with the side of the rail. Check with a combination square that the frame is square and then clamp (or nail) the stiles tightly against the rails. Before you remove the clamps install a 3-inch flat steel corner brace on both sides of each joint to reinforce it.

Before you cut the stile and rail moldings recheck the inside dimension of your frame. Cut the twelve stile moldings to 65 inches in length or to the distance between the frame rails. Make the twelve rail moldings $13\frac{1}{2}$ inches long or cut them to the length of the rail minus $1\frac{1}{2}$ inches.

Next install the moldings to one side of each frame with #3d finishing nails and carpenter's

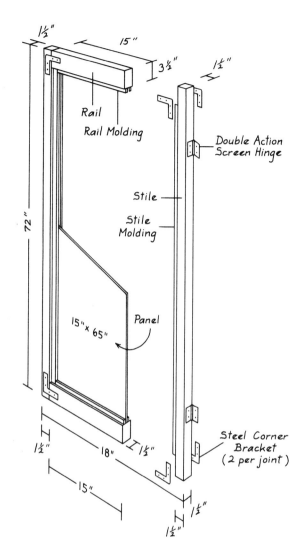

1½"

15"

3½"

1½"

Rail

Rail Molding

Double Action
Screen Hinge

Stile

Stile
Molding

72"

15" x 65"

Panel

Steel Corner
Bracket
(2 per joint)

1½"   18"   1½"

15"

1½"

1½"

you are going to paint or stain both the frame and panel in the same color. Otherwise, it's easier to paint or stain the frame and panels before final assembly.

If you plan to cover the panels with prepasted wallpaper simply cut the wallcovering to overhang all four sides of the panels by about an inch. Then dip the wallcovering in water, let it set a few minutes, and then smooth it on the panel with your hands. Align the patterns so that both sides of all three panels look well together. Use a sharp razor knife to trim the paper flush at the panel edges. Allow the wallpaper to dry overnight.

Final assembly is easy. Place the panels in each of the frames and secure them with the other set of stile and rail moldings. Push the molding tight against the panel and tack them in place with #3d finishing nails but omit the glue. This allows you to remove the panels later if you want to change the wallpaper.

The last step is to connect the three sections with double-action hinges positioned about four inches from the top and bottom of the screen.

glue. Put the stile moldings in place first and then the rail moldings. Note that they are located ⅛ inch in from the edge of the frame.

Cut the three ¼-inch plywood panels to the dimensions shown in the plan or to fit into your frames if they come out a little different in size than ours. Complete the assembly of the screen if

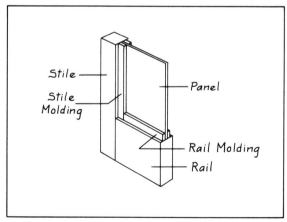

Stile

Stile
Molding

Panel

Rail Molding

Rail

PARTS LIST

To build a 3-panel screen

NAME	AMOUNT	SIZE	MATERIAL
Stile	6	$1\frac{1}{2}'' \times 1\frac{1}{2}'' \times 72''$	pine
Rail	6	$1\frac{1}{2}'' \times 3\frac{1}{2}'' \times 15''$	pine
Stile molding	12	$\frac{1}{2}'' \times \frac{3}{4}'' \times 65''$	pine
Rail molding	12	$\frac{1}{2}'' \times \frac{3}{4}'' \times 13\frac{1}{2}''$	pine
Panel	3	$\frac{1}{4}'' \times 15'' \times 65''$	birch plywood

Materials, Supplies, Tools
To build a 3-panel screen

6 7-foot 2×2 #2 (or better) pine boards
1 8-foot 2×4 #2 (or better) pine board
1 4×8 $\frac{1}{4}$-inch birch plywood panel
2 (sets) $3\frac{1}{8}$-inch double-action hinges (available from 1991 Woodworker's Store, 21801 Industrial Blvd., Rogers, MN 55374-9514, catalog item #29041)
24 3-inch flat steel corner braces
6 sheets #120 grit sandpaper
1 small bottle carpenter's glue
1 small box #3d finishing nails
1 quart paint or stain
1 single roll prepasted wallcovering

hammer
nailset
screwdriver
combination square
measuring tape
handsaw
$\frac{3}{8}$-inch electric drill
razor knife
paintbrush
scissors
2 18-inch clamps or eight-penny finishing nails

Project 14

Make a "Mirror in a Frame"

We found an empty picture frame with a five-dollar price tag at a house sale that turned out to be ideal for framing a hall mirror. Later we priced a new framed mirror that was similar in size and design and found it tagged at a hundred dollars. For a few bucks and about a half hour of work you too can create a similar mirror to use anywhere in your house.

While you're looking at a frame have a measuring tape handy, not only to know its size but also to measure its depth. You can substitute a glass mirror in many wooden frames as long as the recess in the back of the frame is deep enough to hold a piece of glass. Most frames are deep enough, but check to see that there's a recess of at least $1/4$ inch.

The frame should be sturdy, one that is in good structural shape and strong enough to support a glass mirror.

GETTING READY

Prepare the frame to receive the mirror by first removing any nails, brads, or staples from the back. Then give the frame a rubdown with a tack rag to remove any grime. You can leave the hanging wire in place if it's secure.

Measure the length and width of the interior of the recess in the back of the frame. Take these measurements in several different places along both its length and width and then use the smallest of each dimension to know the mirror size needed. This way you will be sure that the mirror will fit into the frame even if it is not perfectly square. If you're not confident measuring for the glass mirror, bring the frame with you to the glass company and they will be happy to size the mirror for you.

A heavy-duty staple gun is a good tool to use to keep the mirror in place. Check the thickness of the frame to see what size staples to use. We were able to use $9/16$-inch-long staples to staple the backing board to the frame. Don't use staples that are too long or they will penetrate the face of the frame. If you use wire brads, drive them into the edge of the frame at an angle with a hammer.

HERE'S HOW

Mounting the mirror in the frame is easy. First, cut a piece of corrugated cardboard and a piece of $1/4$-inch plywood or hardboard backing to fit into the frame. Lay out all the materials on a clean work surface. Place the frame face side down and then put the mirror into it facedown. Next lay the cardboard on top of the back of the mirror in the

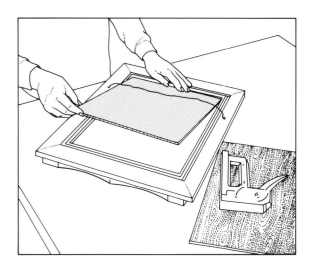

With the front of the frame facedown on the table, lay in a piece of thick cardboard cut to fit exactly.

When the hardboard is secured refasten the old hanging wire and hardware. If you're installing new hanging hardware, position two screw eyes on the back of the frame about four inches down from the top. Make sure that the screw part of the eye is not too long or it will go through the front of the frame.

It is best to use two hanging wires to support a heavy frame and mirror like this one. Twist the end of the hanging wire around one of the eyes and then run it over to the other eye. Leave enough slack in the wire to form a shallow angle, then temporarily wrap the wire around the eye and lead it back to the first eye. Duplicate the slack in the wire so it matches the other one and then cut the wire several inches longer. Unwrap it from the eye and thread it through. Then wrap the wire around the eye several times. Run the wire back to the

frame. The plywood or hardboard backing goes on last. Hold these parts securely in the frame while you pick up the mirror. The mirror should be firmly sandwiched between the backing board and frame. You should not be able to rattle the mirror in the frame. If you can, cut another piece of cardboard and place it between the backing board and mirror.

Check the alignment of the mirror and cardboard, then staple the backing to the frame. Staple the two sides of each corner first, then space the staples every couple of inches around the perimeter of the frame.

If you use wire brads drive them at a slight angle into the side of the recess. Then take a screwdriver and push the brads down tight on the hardboard. Position the brads the same as the staples.

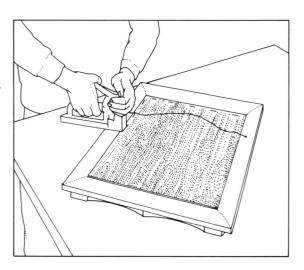

Use a heavy-duty mechanical or electric stapler to attach a piece of hardboard backing to secure the mirror and cardboard permanently.

first eye and secure it by threading it through the
eye and twisting it back on itself.

Materials, Supplies, Tools

frame
mirror and cardboard
$\frac{1}{4}$-inch plywood or hardboard
heavyweight (at least 50-pound) picture hang-
    ing wire and screw eyes
utility knife
hammer
heavy-duty stapler
$\frac{9}{16}$-inch staples
1-inch wire brads
measuring tape

Project 15

Construct a Movable Plant Caddy

If you've ever tried to move a five-foot rubber tree from one room to another or out into the rain for a shower, you'll appreciate this project. Watching a houseplant grow can be very rewarding, but trying to move it can be perilous at best. If you drop it, the damage can be tough on the floor (or your toes) and the severe jolt disturbs the plant's roots. You can damage branches or break off its top growth if you smash it against a wall or doorway. The plant caddy we designed allows you to roll a large plant from one place to another on casters and acts as an appealing cover-up to conceal the plastic container it's growing in.

This wooden plant caddy isn't difficult to construct. It is sized to fit a medium-size pot of about ten inches in diameter. Most lumberyards or home centers carry pine or cedar (or other) $1/4$-inch-thick tongue and groove paneling boards. These boards are light and can be glued together to form the side panels of the caddy. Of course you could use any $1/4$-inch-thick plywood, hardboard, or particle board panel instead. The rest of the caddy is made from readily available dimensional lumber.

GETTING READY

Since all the parts for this project are short you might be able to purchase scrap pieces of wood from the lumberyard instead of whole boards. These are easier to transport and usually cheaper.

When you shop for casters you will find a large selection; choose sturdy ones to support a heavy load. If you're going to roll the caddy over a hardwood or tile floor, purchase casters with rubber tiers.

Cutting all the parts to length is probably the toughest part of this project. We think it is best to cut the parts to size, especially the trim pieces, as you need them. This way you can double-check their measurements. This assures that all the parts fit even if you make the base or some other part slightly oversize. Use the parts list as a guide.

The top trim is joined with mitered joints. The easiest way to cut these joints is with a miter box. You can purchase an inexpensive wood version for less than ten dollars.

HERE'S HOW

Begin by making the bottom from $3/4$-inch plywood, then make the side panels. If you are using individual pieces of tongue and groove lumber, cut them into 14-inch lengths. Edge glue these boards together (four boards per panel) to form the side panels. Make sure that the boards make a panel at least $13^3/4$ inches wide. If the boards glue up wider, trim the panel to size after the glue has dried. If you use plywood or some other sheet material, cut these parts to exact size. Cut the corner braces to length from the 2 × 2 pine stock and the top/bottom rails from 1 × 2 pine.

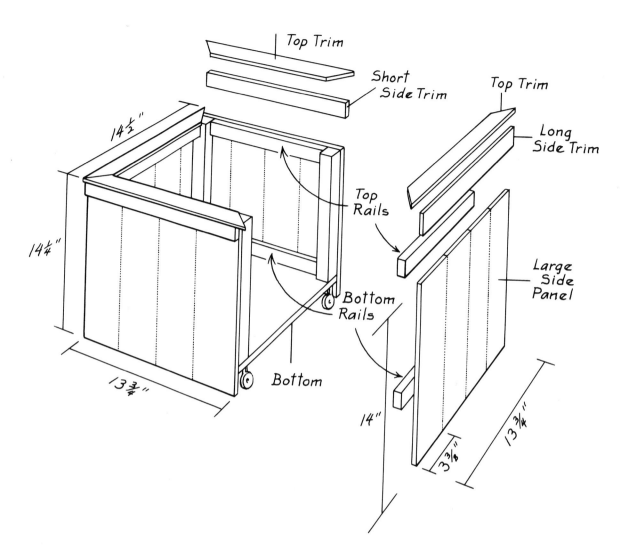

Top Trim

Short Side Trim

Top Trim

Long Side Trim

$14\frac{1}{2}''$

$14\frac{1}{4}''$

Top Rails

Bottom Rails

Large Side Panel

$13\frac{3}{4}''$

Bottom

$14''$

$3\frac{3}{4}''$

$13\frac{3}{4}''$

Choose the best-looking side of each panel assembly and mark it so you can keep it on the outside during assembly. Glue and nail a corner brace on the inside of each panel flush with its top and left edge. Use three or four #3d finishing nails driven through the panel into the corner brace to hold the parts together while the glue sets up. Then glue and nail upper rails to the inside of the panel flush with its top edge. Be sure to put glue on the end of the rail and butt it tight against

the corner brace. Install the lower rails $2\frac{1}{4}$ inches from the bottom of the panel.

Assemble the caddy by gluing and nailing one side assembly to the bottom. Align the corner brace with the edges of the bottom and then nail through the side panel into the edge of the ply-wood bottom. Install the next side assembly in the same way, only put glue on the mating edges of the corner brace and panel. Work your way around the bottom until all four sides are glued and nailed to the bottom and to one another.

Check the outside dimensions of your caddy, then cut the side trim to 14¼ inches or to fit your caddy. Glue and nail it to the outside flush with the top edge. Put the first piece on with its end flush with the left outside edge. Continue around the top gluing and nailing the trim. Cut the pieces for the top trim slightly long. Make a miter cut on one end, then place the piece on the caddy and mark the exact location of the cut on the other end; then cut it. Work your way around the top installing the trim. Turn the unit over and install the casters on the bottom.

You can finish this unit with either a stain covered by a couple of coats of protective varnish or with paint. Either finish is durable. Before you paint or stain, set all the nail heads below the surface of the wood with a nailset and fill these holes with a wood filler. Give the unit a sanding and its ready for the brush.

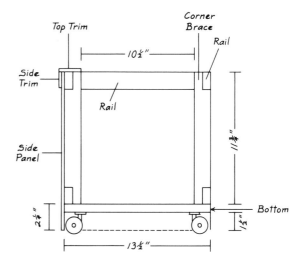

Mount 2-inch casters under plant caddy. Note that side panel hides casters. Bottom is located 1 1/2 inches up from lower edge of unit.

PARTS LIST			
NAME	AMOUNT	SIZE	MATERIAL
Corner brace	4	1½″ × 1½″ × 11¾″	pine
Rail	8	¾″ × 1½″ × 10½″	pine
Bottom	1	¾″ × 13½″ × 13½″	AC plywood
Side panel	4	¼″ × 13¾″ × 14″	pine/plywood panel
Top trim	4	¼″ × 2″ × 14½″	pine lattice
Side trim	4	¼″ × 1½″ × 14¼″	pine lattice
Caster	4	2″	plate mount caster

Materials, Supplies, Tools

6 feet 2 × 2 #2 pine board

8 feet 1 × 2 #2 pine board

6 feet 2-inch pine lattice

6 feet 1½-inch pine lattice

22 feet ¼ × 3½-inch tongue and groove pine
   or cedar paneling

¼ sheet ¾-inch exterior AC grade plywood

4 2-inch plate mount casters with mounting
   screws

1 small bottle carpenter's glue

1 small box #3d finishing nails

4 sheets #120 grit abrasive paper

1 quart paint or stain/finish

wood filler

paintbrush

measuring tape

hammer

screwdriver

nailset

square

hand or circular saw

hand or electric drill and drill bits

miter box

Build a TV/VCR Cart

Your television set and VCR don't have to take up a lot of space or require an expensive piece of furniture to hold them. This cart measures a small 28 inches by 29½ inches by 22 inches deep so it can be tucked into a corner near the handiest outlet. Its compact size makes the cart a nifty addition for storing your home electronics.

The cart is constructed out of a sheet and a half of plywood and it goes together very easily. It's painted and finished off with roller casters so you can move it easily from one place to another. The television set sits on the top shelf with a shelf below for its companion. There is an open back in this area so you can run cords between the sets. The lower section of the unit has a closed back providing ample storage space for videotapes, books, or whatever you decide to store there.

G E T T I N G   R E A D Y

The best way to transport a sheet and a half of plywood is using a car top carrier on top of your car or in the flatbed area behind a pickup truck.

When it comes to cutting the plywood into parts you have a choice between cutting it yourself or having it done at the lumberyard. There's usually a charge for the service, but it's worth checking out the possibility. It makes sense if you don't have a table saw or if your car is too small to handle the load.

If you decide to cut the panels yourself, we think it's easiest to first "rough cut" the parts. Do this by laying out the parts on the large sheet of plywood about an inch more than the actual dimension. Cut them to size and then trim these smaller pieces to their exact dimensions.

While you're at the lumberyard pick up a scrap of 1 × 8 and 1 × 2 lumber to act as spacers to help you in the final assembly of the unit.

H E R E ' S   H O W

Lay out the parts slightly oversize on the plywood sheet with a chalk line. Mark the measurements on the edge of the panel and then stretch the chalk line between the marks. Snap the line to mark the plywood and then cut out the parts from the larger sheet. Then trim the parts to the exact dimensions.

As you cut out the parts you'll notice that the edges of the panels are rough and have voids where small sections of laminate are missing. Fill these voids along all exposed edges with a two-part polyester-based wood filler. Sand the edges smooth after the filler has hardened and then refill any imperfections. Finish off the edges with a good sanding so they're smooth and even.

Assembly is easy if you temporarily install a couple of pieces of scrap lumber to hold the shelves in alignment. Begin by tacking a piece of

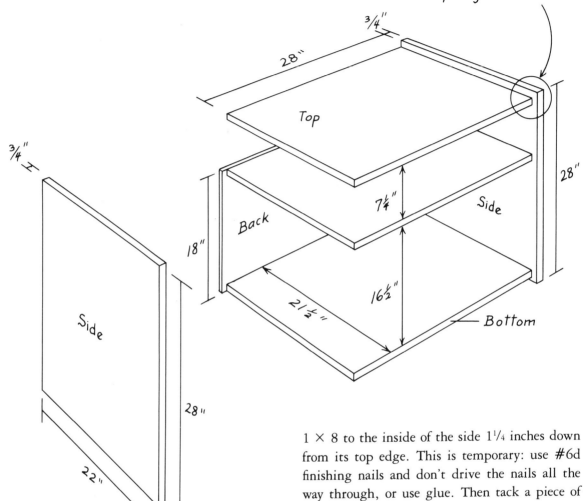

Note ½-inch setback at top edge and front

¾"

28"

Top

3/4"

Side

18"

Back

7¼"

Side

28"

16½"

2½"

Bottom

28"

22"

1 × 8 to the inside of the side 1¼ inches down from its top edge. This is temporary: use #6d finishing nails and don't drive the nails all the way through, or use glue. Then tack a piece of 1 × 2 stock to the bottom inside of the side aligned with its bottom edge.

Apply glue to one end of the top shelf. Place one side panel on a flat surface resting on its back edge and the front edge facing up. Put the top panel into position so that it rests on the upper edge of the spacer and it's in contact with the side. Drive four or five evenly spaced #6d finishing nails through the side into the edge of the top shelf. The side and this shelf should be aligned in the back and be set $1/2$ inch back from the front edge.

Apply glue to the end of the middle shelf and then install it so it rests against the lower edge of the spacer. This shelf and the one you just installed will be $7 1/4$ inches apart. Then install the last shelf (bottom) so that it rests on the lower spacer. This one should be $1 1/2$ inches above the bottom edge of the side.

Remove the spacers from the side and reinstall them on the other side part. Then apply glue to the ends of all three shelf parts and place the side panel in position. Nail it to the shelf ends as you did before.

Turn the unit over so the front is facing down and the back is up. Use a combination square to check that the sides are perpendicular to the shelves. Then apply glue to the back of the middle and bottom shelves and the back edge of each side between these shelves. Place the back in place and align it along all four edges. Then nail it in place with #4d box nails. Turn the unit over and install the casters on the bottom.

Set all the nail heads below the wood surface with a nailset and fill the holes with wood filler.

When the filler is hard, sand smooth and give the rest of the unit a light sanding. Dust the unit thoroughly before applying two coats of enamel paint.

Materials, Supplies, Tools

1 sheet $3/4$-inch birch plywood
$1/2$ sheet $1/4$-inch birch plywood
6 sheets #120 grit abrasive paper
1 small bottle carpenter's glue
1 pint two-part polyester-based wood filler
1 quart alkyd high-gloss enamel
1 small box #6d finishing nails
1 small box #4d box nails
2 sets 2-inch plate mount swivel-base casters
hammer
nailset
combination square
measuring tape
paintbrush
chalk line
hand or circular saw

PARTS LIST			
NAME	AMOUNT	SIZE	MATERIAL
Side	2	$3/4'' \times 22'' \times 28''$	$3/4''$ birch plywood
Shelf	3	$3/4'' \times 28'' \times 21 1/2''$	$3/4''$ birch plywood
Back	1	$1/4'' \times 18'' \times 29 1/2''$	$1/4''$ birch plywood
Caster	4	$2''$	plate mount caster

CHAPTER THREE

Creative Ways
with
Windows and Walls

Project 17

Customize a Plain White Shade

A plain white window shade is just that—dull and ordinary. A simple painted stencil border or a cut-out design are two tricks we use to transform a standard vinyl shade into the focal point of the room.

The pattern we used for the painted gingerbread family stencil came from cookie cutters; we copied the sailboat design from a beach towel. Of course there's any number of designs that you can buy on ready-made stencil sheets at craft stores and art suppliers. These ready-made stencils have a design cut into a sheet of Mylar, which is a heavyweight sheet of plastic. You use these stencils as a pattern to either cut out or paint the design.

GETTING READY

If you're artistic, you can draw your own design and have an original. But if you're like most of us, you'll need help from a greeting card, gift wrapping paper, stationery, or wherever you find a pattern that you like. You might want to carry out a decorating theme in a room by choosing a design from a wallpaper or fabric pattern to use on the shade.

Use the width of the shade as a guide for choosing a design. Whatever the design, it should be centered in the middle of the shade allowing for equal spacing on either end of the design.

Making a stencil is not hard. Remember that simple shapes make easy-to-do stencils, so keep the design as uncomplicated as you can. You need a couple of sheets of semitransparent tracing paper and a sheet of Mylar. These are available in various size sheets from 8 × 12 inches to poster board size. Mylar costs a few dollars and is readily available at artist's supply stores or needlecraft stores specializing in quilting.

To paint the design on the shade you need some acrylic paint and a stencil brush. Both are available at the same stores that sell Mylar and tracing paper.

If the shade is dirty, sponge it clean with a mixture of mild soap and water. Dry the shade with a towel and remove the stiffening bar from the pocket at the end of the shade.

HERE'S HOW

The easiest way to create your own stencil is to trace a design from some other source. First copy a design by placing the tracing paper over it and copying the design onto the tracing paper. Then tape the tracing paper to a piece of cardboard and place the sheet of Mylar over the tracing paper. Cut the shape of the design in the Mylar with an X-acto crafts knife fitted with a new sharp blade. Press down on the Mylar as you cut into it, following the pattern on the tracing paper beneath it. To cut straight lines, hold a metal ruler down tightly against the Mylar and use it to guide the knife

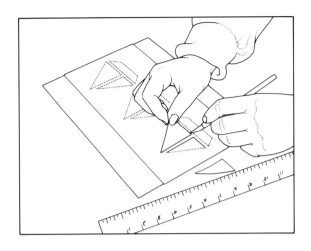

To make your own stencil, use a piece of Mylar and an X-acto crafts knife. Trace the design on a piece of paper and place the Mylar over it, keeping it in place with spray adhesive. Carefully cut out the design in the Mylar using the paper design as a guide.

blade. Make several shallow cuts around the perimeter of the design until you eventually cut completely through the Mylar. Don't try to cut through the tough plastic in a single pass. Make certain that all corners are cut out precisely.

With the cut-out stencil you're ready to begin working on the shade.

If you plan to paint the shade, put down an old sheet or drop cloth to protect your work surface. The easiest way to keep the stencil in place is to temporarily stick it to the shade with spray adhesive. Spray a light coat of adhesive to the back of the stencil just before you position it. Check that the stencil is centered or positioned just the way you want it before you smooth it in place.

Pour the paint into a plastic or paper food tray and then dip the tip of the stencil brush into the paint. Work the excess paint out of the brush by dabbing it on a piece of scrap felt. When the brush

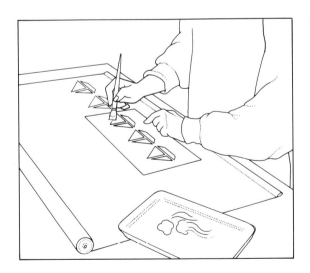

Unroll the window shade on a drop cloth and use spray adhesive to keep the stencil in alignment on it. Dab excess paint onto a scrap of felt before filling in the cut-out stencil area with paint.

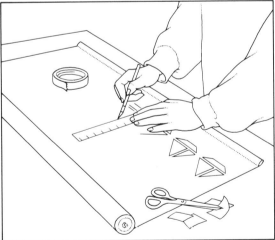

To get sharp, accurate cuts on a stencil design, hold a metal ruler against the straight lines of a design.

is almost dry carefully dab the paint into the cut-out area of the stencil. Don't wipe the brush—use an up-and-down dabbing action. Dab the paint around the outline of the design and then fill in the center area. Dip the brush into the paint when needed.

Fill in all areas of the stencil with paint before removing the stencil and repositioning it. If you're using more than one color of paint and have only one brush, clean out the brush and apply the next color before you move the stencil.

Before you reposition the stencil clean off all paint and respray the back with adhesive.

To cut out a design in a shade, lay the stencil facedown on the backside of the shade. This creates cleaner knife cuts on the front side. Be careful about not damaging the work surface that you're cutting on. Protect it with a piece of heavy cardboard or a piece of $1/4$-inch plywood. Attach the Mylar to the shade using spray adhesive and use an X-acto crafts knife to carefully cut out the stencil design.

Materials, Supplies, Tools

vinyl window shade
precut stencil design or Mylar
tracing paper
masking tape
spray adhesive
acrylic paints, stencil brush
scrap of felt
cardboard
X-acto crafts knife
pencil
metal ruler

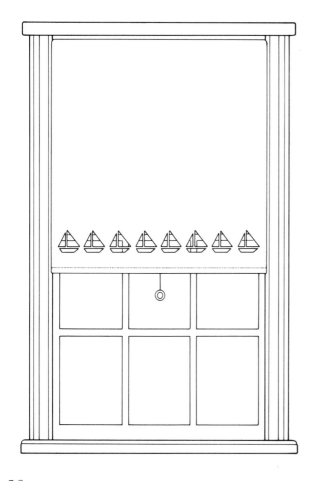

Project 18

Make a Cornice Board

Traditionally a cornice board is constructed of wood and painted or upholstered with fabric to dress up the tops of windows. It does a nice job of hiding drapery hardware and helps save energy by keeping warm air in and cool air outside in the winter.

An upholstered cornice board is a perfect window treatment for any number of decors. In a formal setting it creates a look of richness that crowns traditional draperies or sheers. For a clean, contemporary decor the texture of a fabric-covered cornice softens the starkness of metal blinds or shades. And the warmth of lace panels in a country setting is nicely enhanced by the finishing touch of a cornice board.

If you've ever priced a cornice board you know it can run upwards of $150 to have one built and covered in your favorite fabric. If you have a room full of windows, that mounts up to a hefty investment that's out of reach for many of us.

Here's our solution—a cornice board made of one-inch polystyrene panels that you can build, decorate, and install yourself. We used a Cornice Board Kit, which sells for around twenty dollars and includes all the parts you need. The only thing you add is the fabric of your choice. You could also purchase a sheet of rigid polystyrene insulation board and make your own cornice.

GETTING READY

This kit makes a cornice for a single window that measures 44 inches long, 15 inches high, and 6 inches deep that will fit most windows. To cover the cornice you need a piece of fabric at least 24 inches wide by 64 inches long.

A word about fabric patterns: If you choose fabric with a vertical pattern such as a stripe, you may have to sew two pieces together so the stripes are running up and down and not across the cornice board. If the pattern is solid or a random design, you can use the fabric straight from the bolt.

HERE'S HOW

The cornice board is made from four parts—the front or face board, the two side boards, and the dust board that runs across the top. These four pieces of polystyrene board are glued together to form a lightweight but rigid framework. The foam board is easy to cut with a plain sharp knife or utility knife to fit the exact dimensions of your window.

Assembly of the cornice is easy. Place the pieces of the cornice board on a flat surface. Apply a bead of glue to the edge of the dust board, then position the back of the face board on it so the face board is aligned with its top edge. Glue the sides to the back of the face board and the dust board.

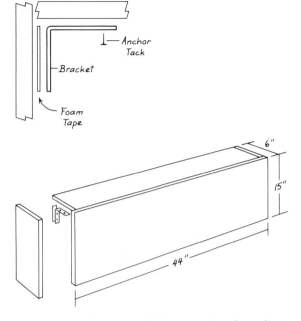

Glue lightweight sections of polystyrene board together to form the cornice base. Unless heavy fabric is used the brackets can be installed with pressure-sensitive foam adhesive tape.

Use masking tape as clamps to hold the parts tightly together while the glue dries. Then let the glue dry for eight hours.

To cover the cornice frame with fabric begin by removing the masking tape. Cut three pieces of polyester batting to fit the face board and two side boards. Apply white glue to the cornice frame and press the batting against the glue and let it dry for about fifteen minutes. You don't have to cover the dust board because it's not visible.

Iron the fabric so it's free of creases and wrinkles. Place it face side down on a flat surface that's larger than the cornice board. Place the cornice board on the backside of the fabric and center it so the fabric pattern is aligned the way you want it.

The fabric is secured to the cornice board at the center of each end board first. Gently pull the fabric taut up and over the edge and secure it into the back side (inside) of the end board with a trim pin. Repeat this on the other end board. Place the pins every few inches so the fabric lies smoothly.

Next work on the face board, beginning at the center and working your way toward the corners. For a smooth fit at the top corners first pin the fabric edges to the dust cover. Then fold the front fabric over the side fabric, easing the excess fabric under to form a 45-degree angle.

Make up the bottom edge corners in the same way. If you're using a thick fabric, you might have some excess that bunches up in the corner. If you do, tuck it inside the cornice and pin it to the inside of the end board.

Two wall brackets hold the cornice board in place. Since the cornice is light the kit comes with a couple of plastic brackets that have a foam adhesive backing. All you have to do is peel the paper off the bracket and stick them on the wall. Align the brackets about two to three inches above and outside the window molding. When you are certain they are in the proper position and level, press them in place. The adhesive on the bracket tape grabs on contact so you get only one chance to position it.

The dust panel of the cornice rests on these brackets. Secure the cornice in place by pushing an anchor tack or pushpin through the bracket up into the dust board. Because of the soft foam board, it's easy to do. This arrangement makes it easy to remove the cornice if you want to clean it.

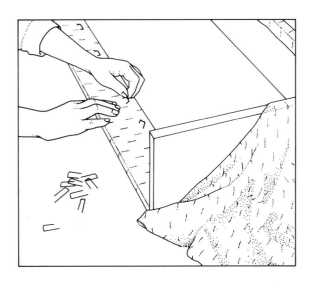

Trim pins secure fabric to the cornice board. At corners where end boards meet the face board, fold the fabric to the inside, creating a smooth crease so the fabric lies smooth.

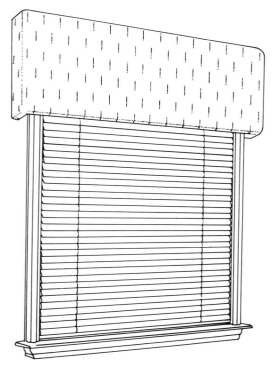

A padded cornice board transforms an ordinary window blind or shade into a designer window treatment.

Materials, Supplies, Tools

Cornice Board Kit
fabric
polyester batting
glue
1-inch-wide masking tape
utility knife
scissors
yardstick
iron
trim pins, pushpins

Source

Cornice Board Kit, Plaid Enterprises
1649 International Blvd.
Norcross, GA 30091-7600

Project 19

Make a Swag Window Topper

A window swag is a draping of soft, loosely folded fabric that makes a simple yet elegant window treatment. Basically you're creating a drape of lined fabric that rests on hardware installed at the top corners of a window. For a clean, contemporary look this window topper is well-suited over miniblinds, shutters, or a shade. You can also use this treatment over full-length sheers or draperies to create a more traditional look.

This window topper is a straightforward sewing project. The mounting hardware is inexpensive and available in most home centers. Using fabric and lining that's 54 inches wide makes the treatment go together easily because it's just the right dimension for creating a swag.

GETTING READY

To figure out how much fabric you need takes a little calculating. Measure how wide you want the swag and how far down the window you want the swag to hang. Add the width of the swag to twice the length of its drop. Then add a foot to this measurement to allow for hemming and draping over the brackets.

To hold the swag in place we used ready-made hardware called EZ Festoon Holders, but there is other hardware available for this type of treatment also. If there's already hardware installed on the wall for existing draperies, look for hardware that's compatible with it. If your swag will be the same size as the existing treatment (such as shades or miniblinds), check that the brackets have slots for the mounting screws instead of holes. Slots allow the bracket to be slipped behind the existing hardware and use the same mounting screws.

HERE'S HOW

To lay out the swag you need a large, clean work surface like a dining room table. The 54-inch width of the fabric and lining doesn't need to be changed; the only cutting required is its length or width across the window. Calculate the length of your swag (see illustration) and cut the fabric and lining to length. Press the fabric and lining flat to remove creases and wrinkles with a clothes iron.

The swag is actually a rectangle with two corners cut off. To create the shape lay down the fabric and lining right sides together. Starting at one corner, measure twelve inches down the short side of the rectangle. Starting there, fold the corner back on itself to form a 45-degree angle. Both sides of the folded back flap should be equal. Go to the other end of the swag and repeat the process. Iron the fold flat, then cut both the fabric and lining along the fold.

Sew the fabric and lining material face sides together with a $1/2$-inch seam allowance. Leave about 36 inches of seam open in the center of the long side so you can turn the fabric and lining inside out. Trim away any excess selvage from all

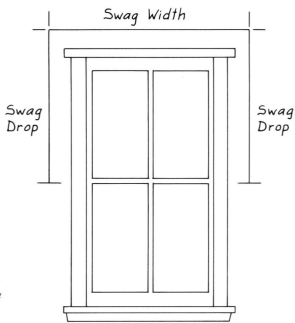

Swag Width

Swag Drop

Swag Drop

Use the window drawing as a guideline when measuring. The drop should extend about halfway down each side of the window.

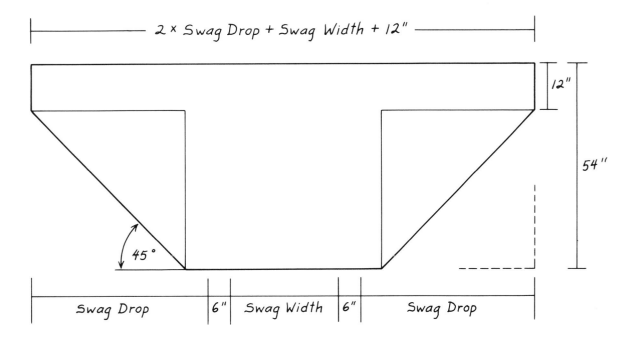

2 × Swag Drop + Swag Width + 12"

12"

54"

45°

Swag Drop | 6" | Swag Width | 6" | Swag Drop

Lay out the fabric and lining material and fold as shown. Cut away the triangular pieces.

63

Position the swag over the brackets so its drops are even and the lowest point of the dip is centered in the window.

seams and then turn the swag inside out so the face side of both fabric and lining is showing. Press all of the seams flat and then hand stitch the open seam so it's closed.

Mount the brackets on the window casing or wall. If there is already hardware in place to support shades, blinds, or drapes, loosen the mounting screws holding them in place and slip the swag bracket under the bracket and tighten the screws. You can also fasten the brackets directly in the walls with plastic wall anchors.

Loosely hold the fabric in both hands and position it on the support arms of the brackets so it's evenly spaced. You'll have to play around with the swag to get it to drape properly in the center. Work from the center out to the sides, gently gathering and pleating the fabric so it lies smoothly. Stand back from the window to get an overall view until you're satisfied with how the swag falls.

Materials, Supplies, Tools

54-inch fabric and lining
matching thread
chalk
round hardware brackets
sewing machine
screwdriver
measuring tape
scissors
iron

Source

EZ Festoon Holder, Stanley Kleiman Co., Inc.
1119 W. St. Georges Ave.
Linden, NJ 07036

Project 20

Install a String Wall Cover-up

Here's an interesting trick for a wall cover-up that has an unusual rustic appeal. Jute string is strung up and down the wall to create a rich, textured look. We've seen this done very effectively in a home office and on a single wall of a den decorated with artwork. This wall treatment is deceptively simple. It involves running string up and down a wall, securing it around small nails at the top and bottom of the wall.

The installation is as simple as nailing a few hundred brads along the top and bottom of a wall. That's the tedious part of the project. The fun part begins when you run the string up and down the wall, which instantly changes its look.

G E T T I N G   R E A D Y

To estimate how much string and how many nails are needed for a wall use these figures as a guideline. A 190-foot roll of string will cover 5–6 linear inches of wall. To cover an average 8-foot-long wall (with an 8-foot high ceiling), it will take 16–17 rolls of string. The wire brads are spaced about ¼ inch apart so figure about 100 nails per linear foot.

H E R E ' S   H O W

First, remove any dust from the walls, ceiling, and baseboard woodwork before beginning to nail. Begin by nailing the brads closely together along the top of the wall and then along the bottom just above the baseboard molding. Work on a ladder at the top of the wall and place the first nail as close to the ceiling as possible. To gauge the spacing between the next and subsequent nails place it about ⅛ inch to ¼ inch apart. Use the tip of your little finger as a spacer; it's your handiest gauge.

Leave the brad heads protruding about ¾ inch out of the wall. Drive them well into the wall but don't pound them in too far or you will have a hard time wrapping the string around them. When you have about a foot of nails along the top of the wall, repeat the procedure at the bottom. Try to align the top and bottom rows of nails with each other, but keep in mind that you are not going to get them perfect. It is important to keep the nail count at the top and bottom the same.

Begin stringing the wall by tying a simple knot at the end of the string around the first nail at the bottom of the wall. Pull the string up the wall to the nail above it. Wrap it around the nail and then stretch it back down to the bottom row of nails. Repeat this process until you run out of

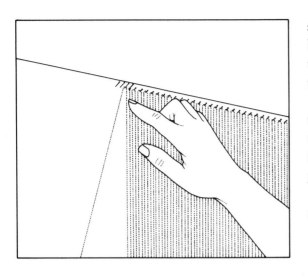

string. Plan to end at the bottom and start a new ball of string by tying off the end of the old ball to a bottom nail and starting the new one from this nail.

When you have completed running the string up and down the wall, go back and carefully tap the nails into the wall so they protrude about a $1/4$ inch. Don't drive them too far in or the string will pop off and you will have a real mess.

To hang artwork simply separate the string to nail the hanger into the wall.

As you begin a new roll of string, tie a knot around the nail head to secure it in place. Then continue running the string up and down the wall.

Materials, Supplies, Tools

jute string
brads
measuring tape
hammer (an upholstery or kid's hammer
    preferred)
ladder

To wrap the string around the nail head, gently push the string flat against the wall to keep it taut and secure.

Project 21

Create a Wall Molding Picture Gallery

Art galleries have known for decades that the clean, uncluttered look of a plain wall is the ideal backdrop for pieces of art. Instead of mounting framed artwork directly to the wall, it's often placed on a ledge or narrow shelf so it can be easily moved as exhibits change. Here's our version—a do-it-yourself art gallery for displaying pictures and artwork at home. Use it to showcase the kids' artwork, if not your own. You don't have to build just one ledge. If you have numerous paintings, consider installing two or three ledges of the same length.

Using only two pieces of simple pine lattice, you can cut your own picture gallery to whatever length is suitable for your room. Ours is 8 feet long and protrudes out $1^3/_4$ inches from the wall. A thin piece of lattice trim acts as a lip so the artwork doesn't slip off the ledge.

Finished in a semigloss paint to match the window and door trim, this shelf becomes an integral part of the room.

GETTING READY

Most lumberyards carry a wide selection of lattices and moldings. You can substitute a piece of molding for the front trim instead of the lattice we used. Whatever you decide, investigate the lumber before you purchase it. Look down its length and make sure that it's not bowed, twisted, or warped.

Our directions are for an 8-foot art ledge. Make adjustments to the length depending on how long you want yours to be. We recommend that you mount the ledge to your wall by screwing it directly to the wall studs. If you will not be setting heavy framed pictures on the rail, you can use plastic wall anchors, but space them at least every 12 inches instead of the 16 inches we specify for stud mounting.

HERE'S HOW

This is a very easy project because all you have to do is drill seven $1/_4$-inch holes on 16-inch centers (that means measured 16 inches apart) through the edge of an 8-foot section of 1 × 2 pine stock. Use a countersink bit to enlarge the holes on one side of the board so the screw heads will be recessed and flush with the face side of the board.

Sand the ledge board and the 8-foot section of $1^3/_8$-inch-wide lattice smooth. Then give both pieces a priming coat of paint, followed by a top coat of semi-enamel paint when the primer has dried.

Attach the ledge board to the wall with $3^1/_2$-inch #8 FH wood screws driven into the wall studs. Then nail the lattice trim to the front of the ledge board with 1-inch wire brads spaced on 12-inch centers. The lattice trim hides the screws and provides a lip to prevent the pictures from falling off the ledge board.

PARTS LIST			
NAME	AMOUNT	SIZE	MATERIAL
Ledge	1	$3/4'' \times 1 1/2'' \times 8'$	pine
Trim	1	$1/4'' \times 1 3/8'' \times 8'$	pine lattice

Materials, Supplies, Tools

8-foot 1 x 2 pine
8-foot $1 3/8$-inch pine lattice
6 $3 1/2$-inch #8 FH wood screws (or 6 plastic
  wall anchors)
1 small box 1-inch wire brads
1 sheet #120 grit abrasive paper
1 pint primer and paint, brushes
hammer
nailset
hand or circular saw
drill and drill bits
screwdriver

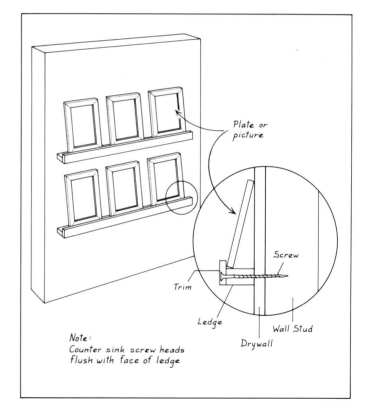

Plate or picture

Screw

Trim

Ledge

Drywall

Wall Stud

Note:
Counter sink screw heads
flush with face of ledge

Install Ornamental Wood Brackets

Many newer houses lack the elaborate moldings and trim that grace older homes. If you have a plain-Jane house and would like to dress it up, consider installing ornamental woodwork on the casework in the corners of passageways between living rooms or hallways.

On a quick trip through your local lumberyard or home center you will discover a choice of brackets and other trim items. Another source for ornamental woodwork is through the growing number of mail order catalogue retailers that specialize in "gingerbread trim," as it's often called.

This project deals with installing a decorative bracket, but the installation process is basically the same for all wooden brackets. It doesn't matter if it's a corner bracket in the living room or an elaborate Victorian bracket on your front porch.

To trim out the entrance to a room with these inexpensive brackets will take less than an hour. Of course you will have to spend some more time painting or staining it but the installation is a quickie.

GETTING READY

The Victorian bracket we chose measures six inches on each side, so it should be mounted in a wide opening. We chose a doorway between a living and dining room. Brackets like this can be placed just about anywhere, but shouldn't obstruct the opening of the door itself. There are brackets available in all sizes that will fit just about anywhere.

HERE'S HOW

Installing these brackets or other ready-made trim is easy. Unless you plan to paint the woodwork after the bracket is installed, you will find it easier to finish the brackets or trim before you install it.

The brackets we used were made from pine and came sanded fairly smooth right out of the package. Pine and other soft woods do not take stain very well unless the wood is uniformly sanded, especially the end grain. Before you stain these brackets give them a sanding and concentrate on the end grain areas, especially the curved areas.

After sanding apply stain or paint the brackets. Leave the back of the base (side mounted against the wall) bare so the finish will not interfere with the adhesive.

When the finish is dry, drive a couple of #4d finishing nails through the base of the bracket so the point of the nails just starts to come out the back of the bracket. You can mount small brackets with nails only but use adhesive on larger ones. Apply a bead of adhesive down the center of the bracket back. Place the bracket in position and push it tight against the casework. Drive the nails

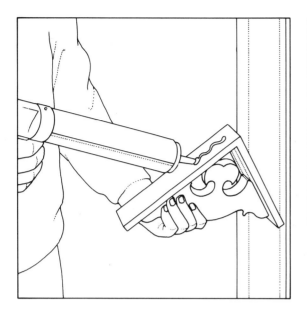

Apply a thin bead of adhesive to the back of the bracket. Keep the adhesive in the center part of the bracket so it will not be squeezed out onto the casework.

Place the bracket in position, holding it in place with finishing nails until the adhesive sets. Either remove the nails or set their heads with a nailset and fill the depression with wood filler.

through the bracket into the trim to hold the bracket in place while the adhesive sets up.

If adhesive is pushed out the sides of the bracket, look on the tube for cleanup directions. Most adhesives will wipe up with a damp rag or a tack rag. In either case clean up the adhesive before it sets up.

Materials, Supplies, Tools

decorative brackets
tube construction adhesive
1 small box #4d finishing nails
3 sheets #120 grit abrasive paper
1 pint polyurethane varnish
caulking gun
measuring tape
hammer
nailset
paintbrush

Project 23

Create a Patchwork Wall

Here's a camouflage trick that will disguise an ugly wall and requires only two things: scraps of fabric and clear wallpaper adhesive. This hodge-podge of colors, textures, and designs also makes a colorful solution to a dull room. It's also an interesting treatment for an alcove or along a hallway. It's especially attractive in a room with a white ceiling and trim paint. This project works best on smooth gypsum wallboard (drywall) or plaster walls, but there's no reason it can't conceal unwanted paneling, too.

GETTING READY

One of the appeals of a patchwork quilt is the array of colors and patterns, and that's true for this wall treatment as well. Use as many fabrics with different patterns and colors as you can and cut them in a variety of sizes and shapes. The more sizes and shapes, the better.

On the hall wall we covered we used squares ranging from four inches up to eight inches and rectangles of various shapes. Proportion the size of patches to the wall or room. For example, if you're decorating a small room or alcove, cut smaller-size patches so they're scaled to the space.

To estimate how much fabric you'll need to patchwork a wall, measure the length and the width of the wall and multiply these two numbers together. That gives you the entire surface area to be covered. Let's say the wall is 8 feet high by 10

feet long; it will have 80 square feet of surface area. Since you will not be covering doors or windows, subtract the area of these openings from the total. Use 21 square feet for an average-size door and 15 square feet for each window. That makes it 36 square feet of wall space you will not cover with fabric, so you have to have at least 44 square feet of fabric patches.

It's better to cut too many squares and rectangles of fabric instead of too few, so as you're creating your patchwork you'll have a wide selection of fabric to choose from. You can also overlap some of the squares for different effects, so cut more scraps than you think you'll need.

Use a pair of pinking shears to cut fabric patches in squares and rectangles. Give the fabric a quick press with a clothes iron so it lays smoothly for cutting.

Before you cover any wall remove any dust or cobwebs from the surface, and if it's dirty wash it down with an all-purpose cleaner.

HERE'S HOW

Begin at the top of the wall and apply clear wallpaper adhesive to an area about 18 inches square. Lay on the first fabric patch in the top corner section of the wall. Smooth it out onto the adhesive so it lies flat. Butt the edge of the fabric into the corner and against the ceiling. Apply the next fabric patch, overlapping the edges by about a ¼ inch. Mix and match the colors and patterns so there's a contrast between them.

If you're working from a ladder, apply the fabric patches over as much of the wall area as you can within a comfortable reach. Be careful not to overextend yourself on the ladder; get down from the ladder and move it into position so you'll avoid tipping the ladder and possibly falling.

At casings around windows or doors you'll have to trim the patches to fit. Hold a fabric patch in position and determine about how much should be cut away so the patch will lie flat against the trim. At corners the patch has to have a relief cut made at the point of the corner trim so it will lay flat. With the patch in place make a 45-degree relief cut starting at the corner of the molding outward to the end of the patch. Two sides of the patch can then be folded back so it lies against the trim.

Allow the adhesive to dry before you trim away any excess fabric from molding or casing with a sharp knife. Trim the patches at the ceiling and along the baseboard in the same way.

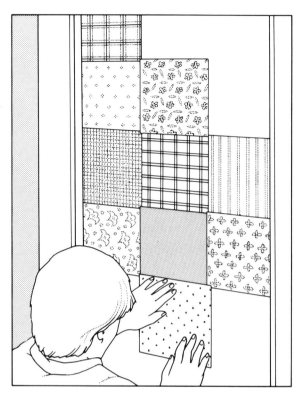

Use a foam applicator to apply clear wallpaper adhesive to the wall and then lay fabric patch onto it. Smooth the fabric so it lies flat and overlaps adjoining patches by about ¹/₄ inch.

Materials, Supplies, Tools

fabric scraps
clear wallpaper adhesive
foam applicator
pinking shears
razor or craft knife
measuring tape
iron
ladder (if needed)

Project 24

Make Cut-out Wall Borders

If you can wield a pair of scissors, you can create a custom-designed wall border that makes short work of decorating a room. Instead of using a traditional wallpaper border that requires adhesives, we made our own border using self-adhesive decorative covering. For years this product was relegated to lining pantry and cabinet shelves, but today it's available in a wide selection of colors and patterns for various uses.

This project can transform a kid's room with ordinary painted walls into a cheerful, colorful area in just a few hours. Use the idea to create a chair rail effect around a bathroom, kitchen, or anywhere that you'd like to add interest and color in a room.

We've shown two ideas for a kid's room. For the alphabet border we used a solid color decorative covering and letters cut out from a set of 6-inch Gothic stencils, which you'll find in most office supply stores. To set off the design we used two strips of colorful tape; one was ³/₄ inch, the other ¹/₄ inch wide.

For an even easier border treatment we cut felt decorative paper covering into pennants and used 1-inch-wide cloth tape to tie the pennants together. Other possibilities include a fleet of sailboats or a train of railroad cars. For these and any other designs requiring a pattern, trace them from drawings on wrapping paper, a greeting card, or even a coloring book.

GETTING READY

To estimate how many feet of a design you'll need, measure the perimeter of the room by adding the lengths of each wall together. A typical rectangular 10 × 15 foot room will have a perimeter of 50 feet. That means you'll need 50 feet (or 600 inches) of a border design to decorate the walls.

The alphabet stencils we used have letters that are 4 inches wide. Figuring there's an inch of space between each letter, we figured each letter will take 5 inches and we'd need 120 letters. This is a ballpark estimate because each room is different and you have to make allowances for corners and other obstructions (i.e., an exposed pipe) that wouldn't be covered.

To estimate the number of pennants, you will need to find the perimeter of your room and divide the figure by the width of the pennant. For example, let's say your room had a perimeter of 70 feet (or 840 inches) and your pennant pattern was 8¹/₂ inches wide at the top and 10¹/₂ inches long. There's no space in between the pennants so we divided 8¹/₂ inches into 840 inches to find that we needed approximately 100 pennants to decorate the room. Simply purchase enough tape to reach around the perimeter of the room.

To prepare the walls for decoration give them a quick once-over with a dust mop or rag to remove any cobwebs or dust. If the walls are dirty, wash them down so the adhesive covering has a clean surface to adhere to.

HERE'S HOW

Whatever shape you decide to use, trace it on the back of the Con-Tact paper. By tracing on the back the pencil layout lines are drawn on peel-away backing so there are no pencil marks left on the face of the paper. Lay the Con-Tact paper face side down on a flat working surface and put the stencil or pattern on top of it face side down. If you are tracing letters, be sure you put the stencil face side down so the letters appear backward as you trace their shapes on the back of the Con-Tact paper.

The letters require a guideline so the design will be straight on the wall. The easiest way to do this is with a chalk line. This is a handheld gizmo that's filled with string and chalk. A chalk line costs about five dollars and is available in hardware stores and home centers. What makes this gadget handy is a clip at the end of the string that you can hook over a wall corner or a small finishing nail so it takes only one person to make a long, straight line.

To snap the layout line for the letters 12 inches below the ceiling measure down 12 inches from the ceiling at each end of the wall and mark this point with a light pencil mark. Drive a small finishing nail through one of these marks, then hook the end of the chalk line over it and stretch it tight to the mark at the other end of the room. Gently pluck the line and the chalk will mark the wall. Do this on all the walls in the room.

Unroll the ¾-inch tape and apply it on the wall so that it covers the chalk line. Where two

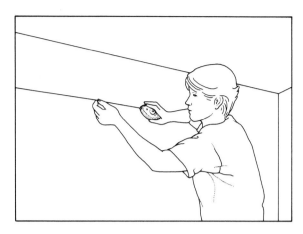

Measure down 12 inches from the ceiling and make several marks on the wall. Then run a chalk line through the marks for a continual straight line around the room.

Use the cut-out stencil sheet as a guide for placing letters on the wall.

pieces of tape meet, overlap the pieces by about an inch, then cut through both layers of tape with a sharp razor or utility knife to make a butt joint. Peel away the cut-off ends and smooth the tape. When that's completed apply the thinner tape just beneath it.

We found that using the stencil as a guide helped align the stick-on letters. Hold the stencil up to the wall to help you figure where the letter should be placed. We taped the stencil temporarily in place and then filled in the spaces with the cut-out pieces. Press the pieces lightly into place at first so you can adjust them if necessary. When they're properly aligned on the wall firmly smooth them in place.

The pennants touch each other on both sides to create the look of a long row of colorful flags attached together. Apply the pennants by first snapping a chalk line a $1/2$ inch below the ceiling. Align the pennants with the chalk line. When they are all in place cover the chalk line and the top of the pennants with $3/4$-inch tape. Check the tape alignment before you press it firmly in place.

Materials, Supplies, Tools

adhesive-backed decorative paper
stencils or cardboard pattern
cloth tape in various sizes
scissors
measuring tape
chalk line
pencil

Sources

Letter stencils: E-Z Letter Quik Stik Co.
P. O. Box 829
Westminster, MD 21157
Con-Tact self-adhesive decorative covering
Rubbermaid Inc.
1147 Akron Rd.
Wooster, OH 44691

Create a different look in a room using colorful pennants hung from a strip of $3/4$-inch tape.

CHAPTER FOUR

Kitchen and Bathroom Magic

Project 25

Rejuvenate a Butcher Block

The rich natural look of butcher block makes it a popular choice for furniture, kitchen counters, and chopping blocks. Technically butcher block is the end grain of hardwood that has been laminated together, but that definition doesn't begin to describe its handsome and durable surface. In most instances, a butcher block surface is finished in a "wipe-on-oil," which means that it's easily restorable after use and abuse.

Whether it's a knife-scarred chopping block or the tabletop in the family room, the procedure to rejuvenate a well-worn butcher block surface remains the same. The difference is the amount of work required to sand away the imperfections. If the surface is severely marred by deep knife gouges or burn marks, it will require more sanding than a butcher block surface that's simply embedded with dirt and grease. That's the bull work of this project; the fun part is finishing the new surface with an easy wipe-on oil finish. If the butcher block is in the kitchen where food is involved, use mineral oil. It's the only completely safe, nontoxic finish that we know of that gives good-looking results. If the butcher block is on a tabletop, use tung oil for a durable wipe-on finish that gives long-lasting protection.

GETTING READY

When you're working on a piece of furniture with a butcher block top, position it on a drop cloth to protect the floor and clear away other furnishings so you can walk around it. Use a floor lamp or clip-on lights so you'll be able to see what you're doing.

When you're rejuvenating a butcher block chopping block or sandwich board insert in a kitchen countertop, protect the backsplash and adjoining countertop with two layers of one-inch or wider masking tape. This is important if you don't want to cause damage while you're sanding and scraping.

HERE'S HOW

If the butcher block is not damaged or stained, use a medium grade #120 grit abrasive sandpaper to sand off the top layer of finish. Use either a sanding block or an electric hand sander (called a palm sander) to lightly peel off this layer, which leaves a porous surface for the new oil finish to adhere to.

For damaged or stained butcher block begin by scraping off the top layer of finish with a hook or wood scraper. Pull the scraper toward you as you peel away the top layer to expose the wood below. Then sand the butcher block with a medium grade sandpaper and repeat the process as many times as it's necessary to remove the top layer of finish. If a burn mark or ring of stain doesn't budge, you could try to bleach it out with household bleach.

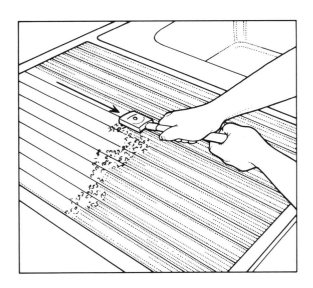

A wood scraper lets you remove the top layer of finish by scraping it off the surface. Hold the scraper firmly in both hands and pull it toward you.

Ordinary mineral oil is a popular finish for butcher block that comes in contact with food; tung oil is an ideal choice for finishing the butcher block tops of furniture.

79

Use a small brush to apply a solution of half warm water and half bleach to the stained area. Let it set for about ten minutes to see if it lightens the area. If not, reapply the bleach solution as many times as necessary. You also might try using the bleach full strength on stubborn areas.

When the area lightens, neutralize the bleach with a solution of equal parts household vinegar and water. Then wash the surface with a solution of mild soap and water and let it dry thoroughly. When the area has dried completely, sand the entire butcher block surface to a consistent smoothness.

To finish a butcher block tabletop use tung oil with a rag. Gently apply the finish by rubbing it into the unfinished wood. When it's dry, buff it to a tough protective finish.

Use mineral oil on any butcher block surface where food is involved, such as a chopping block or sandwich board. Pour the oil into a clean rag and rub it into the butcher block. Several applications are usually needed because the raw wood soaks up the oil. After each application of mineral oil, buff it dry with a clean, dry rag.

Materials, Supplies, Tools

household bleach
household vinegar and water
mild soap and water
tung or mineral oil
drop cloth (old sheet, blanket, draperies)
masking tape
rags, sponge
electric sander
sanding block
hook or wood scraper
small brush (i.e., toothbrush, nailbrush)
rubber gloves

Source

Tung Oil Finish, Minwax Company Inc.
15 Mercedes Dr.
Montvale, NJ 07645

Project 26

Build a Wineglass Rack

We've seen racks for stemmed glassware that are designed for installation below a cabinet, but when stored outside of a cabinet the glass is exposed to possible damage and dirt. We prefer to store stemware *inside* a cabinet with these easy-to-make racks you can customize to fit the interior of your cabinet. Because the glasses hang upside down from the top of a shelf they're easily accessible, stay clean inside, are safe from being knocked over, and don't take up a lot of space.

The rack is a module 18 inches long and $3\frac{1}{2}$ inches wide that holds a single row of glasses. To store a glass, turn it upside down, slide its base into the channel, and push it to the back of the rack. The rack will hold a glass with a base up to $2\frac{1}{2}$ inches wide, which should accommodate most of your stemware. The size of your glasses determines the number of glasses that will fit into each rack module. Since the modules are self-contained, you can make one or as many as you need.

If you're undecided about which cabinet should be designated for stemware, consider the height of the glasses. If you have cabinets with removable shelves, you can reposition the shelves so they'll hold your tallest glassware. But if the shelves are stationary, you're limited to what's available. Also consider where in the kitchen you want to locate glassware. If you don't use stemware often, consider an out-of-the-way cabinet, one that's not readily accessible. If you use stemware daily, choose a cabinet that's near the kitchen sink and dishwasher so you can transfer them easily and safely.

GETTING READY

The modules are made from pine lattice and baluster stock, which are both available at most lumberyards or home centers. If they don't stock the wide lattice, you can substitute a common 1 × 4 pine stock. It is the same width but it's thicker than the lattice.

The racks are mounted to the underside of the shelves or the bottom of the cabinet. Check the thickness of your shelves. Most are at least $\frac{1}{2}$ inch thick so the $\frac{5}{8}$-inch-long screws we specify will not come out the top side of the shelf. If your shelves are thinner, purchase screws that aren't longer than the combined thickness of the rack base and shelf.

HERE'S HOW

Cut the base, cleats, and flanges about two inches shorter than the inside depth of your cabinet. Apply glue to the cleats and nail them flush with the outside edge and ends of the base with 1-inch wire brads. Nail and glue the flanges to these cleats.

When the glue is dry chip away any glue that has been pushed out of the joints and then sand the rack smooth. These modules are hung from the underside of the shelves with four ⅝-inch-long #8 flat head wood screws. Drill four evenly spaced ¼-inch pilot holes along the center of the base for these screws. Countersink the pilot holes so the screwheads lie flush with the surface of the module's base.

The rack can remain natural; you can also paint or stain it before you put it into place.

When the finish is dry place the rack in position inside the cabinet and use a pencil placed through the pilot holes to mark the location of the pilot holes you have to drill in the shelf. Make these pilot holes ⅛ inch in diameter and be careful not to drill completely through the shelf.

Mount the modules with the #8 screws.

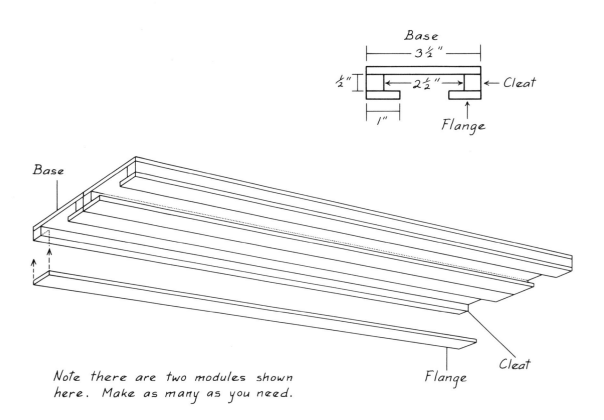

Note there are two modules shown here. Make as many as you need.

PARTS LIST			
To make one module			
NAME	AMOUNT	SIZE	MATERIAL
Base	1	$\frac{1}{4}'' \times 3\frac{1}{2}'' \times 18''$	pine lattice
Cleat	2	$\frac{1}{2}'' \times \frac{1}{2}'' \times 18''$	pine baluster
Flange	2	$\frac{1}{4}'' \times 1'' \times 18''$	pine lattice

Materials, Supplies, Tools

To make one module

1 18-inch 3½-inch pine lattice
1 3-foot 1-inch pine lattice
1 3-foot ½ × ½-inch baluster pine stock
1 small bottle carpenter's glue
1 small box 1-inch wire brads
⅝-inch-long #8 flat head wood screws
2 sheets #120 grit abrasive paper
1 pint polyurethane varnish

measuring tape
hammer
screwdriver
nailset
hand or circular saw
hand or electric drill and bits
paintbrush

Project 27

Make a Bed Sheet Shower Curtain

You can make your own shower curtain out of a flat double bed sheet, giving you a much wider choice of colors, patterns, and styles than what's offered in the bath shop section of your local stores—not to mention saving a significant amount of money. If you want to coordinate a bedroom and bathroom, this project makes it easy. Hung with a plastic shower liner, a bed sheet shower curtain can be washed and reused for many years.

To highlight the top of the curtain with a valance, choose a bed sheet with a border pattern. This might be a contrasting band of fabric, a lace border, or a row of ruffles at the head of the sheet. We chose a plain white percale sheet with an eyelet border.

Our curtain consists of the shower curtain and a valance made from a flat double bed sheet measuring approximately 81 × 96 inches. To give the curtain strength and structure along the top, buckram heading tape is sewn in between the two layers of fabric. The bottom of the sheet is already hemmed so there's a minimum of sewing required to make the curtain and valance. Only a small amount of the sheet goes unused to make a 70-inch-square curtain.

GETTING READY

When you're buying the sheet also purchase a clear or white vinyl shower curtain liner along with a package of shower curtain rings, which come in packages of twelve.

Wash and dry the sheet and lightly press it with a clothes iron.

HERE'S HOW

Begin by cutting the two sides of the curtain so it measures 74 inches wide. Each side has a 1-inch double-fold hem, so turn under a 1-inch hem, press the fold flat, and then turn it again and press the hem flat. Do the same to the other side and then run both through your sewing machine, using a straight stitch hem edge.

Next, measure 71 inches up from the hemmed bottom, which allows for a finished dimension of 70 inches plus a 1-inch hem allowance. Cut off the top part of the sheet with the border and set it aside. Turn under the 1-inch hem allowance at the top of the curtain and press it flat.

Cut the border valance so that it measures 18 inches up from the bottom of the border. This allows for a finished height of 17 inches plus a 1-inch hem allowance at the top. Fold over the hem allowance at the top of the valance and press it flat.

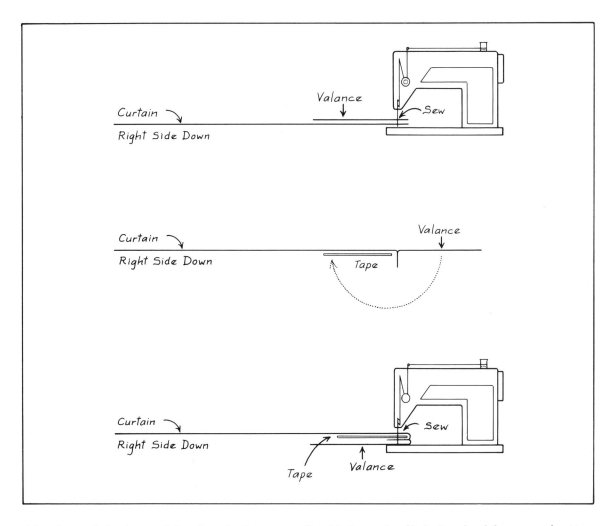

Place the curtain facedown and the valance facedown on top of it with the top edge of both aligned and then sew together. Next place heading at top of curtain and fold over valance. Sew curtain, tape, and valance together.

On a flat surface lay out the curtain and valance. Place the right side of the valance against the back of the curtain. Sew the top of the curtain to the top of the valance with a 1-inch seam allowance. Turn the pieces so that the curtain is right side up and press the seam flat toward the body of the curtain. Cut the heading tape to 69 inches and align it along the top of the curtain.

Check that it lies flat and is placed against the right side of the curtain; it should be set back about ½ inch from each side of the curtain.

Fold the valance over the tape and press the top seam flat. Sew the top side edges of curtain, heading tape, and valance together. Then run the top of the curtain and valance through your machine and keep the seam about ½ inch from the top. Run another stitch about 3½ inches down from the top to secure the bottom of the heading tape.

Use your button hole attachment to make twelve 1-inch button holes along the top to hold the curtain rings. Locate the holes in the curtain to match the plastic liner so they will be aligned when they hang together.

Press the shower curtain and valance and then hang it with the plastic liner.

Materials, Supplies, Tools

1 unfitted double bed sheet with border
matching thread
1 white vinyl shower curtain
1 package of 12 shower curtain rings
6 feet of buckram heading tape (approx. 3½ inches wide)
sewing machine with button hole attachment
scissors
measuring tape
iron

Project 28

Install a Shower Curtain Rod

An expansion-type shower curtain rod is the quickest way to hang a shower curtain, but if you have ever used one you know its shortcomings. If anyone accidentaliy leans against the curtain just slightly, that's all it takes to make the rod and curtain come tumbling down.

Our best advice is to install an honest-to-goodness shower curtain rod that is securely mounted to the wall. It will be there forever and won't be a short-term addition. This type of rod is easy to install even if you have to do it in ceramic tile.

GETTING READY

For ten dollars you can purchase a shower rod and the mounting hardware. In addition to this purchase pick up a package of small plastic wall anchors (you'll need four) and a carbide-tipped masonry bit to drill the pilot holes into ceramic tile. Look on the anchor package to find out what size drill is needed. Small anchors usually require at least a $3/16$-inch or $1/4$-inch hole. If you don't have any tape, purchase a roll of masking tape; otherwise, you can use just about any kind of tape that you already have on hand.

HERE'S HOW

Since most shower curtains are approximately 70 inches long, you will want to mount the rod about 65 inches above the top of the tub so the shower curtain hangs into it. Check that there is no conflict with the ceiling. Some bathtubs have a dropped ceiling or soffit over the area.

Put several strips of tape to cover the area where the rod hardware will be installed to make drilling the pilot holes into the hard tile surface easier. Then mark the location of the rod center on the tape. Center the rod hardware over the mark and use it as a template to mark the location of the mounting screw pilot holes. Put the point of your pencil through the screw holes in the bracket to transfer the location of the pilot holes to the tape. Repeat this process on the other wall.

To position the other bracket so that the rod will be level insert the rod in the installed bracket and hold a level on top of it. Adjust the rod and then mark the location for the second bracket.

The most difficult part of drilling a hole in tile is keeping the drill bit from wandering off the mark while starting the hole. The tape helps hold the drill in place until the bit bites into the hard, glassy surface. If you have a variable speed drill, start drilling very slowly. Hold the drill square to the wall to keep the bit from wandering as you

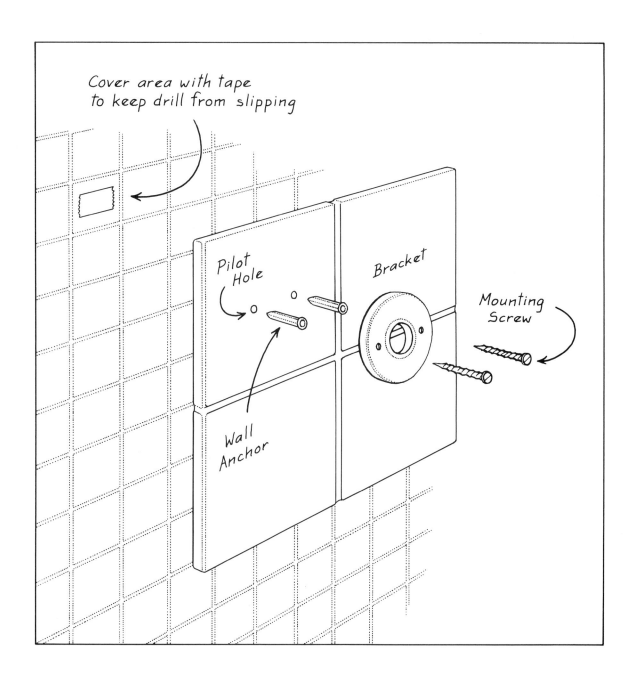

Cover area with tape
to keep drill from slipping

Pilot
Hole

Bracket

Mounting
Screw

Wall
Anchor

drill. Drill the holes completely through the tile and wallboard or at least deep enough so the wall anchors will not bottom in the hole.

After the holes are made remove the tape and insert the plastic anchors into the pilot holes. Push them in as far as they will go by hand and then tap them in place with a hammer. Don't hammer too hard and be careful not to miss the anchor and crack the tile with the hammer.

Place one mounting bracket over the anchors and install the screws. Don't tighten them all the way until the other bracket is in place. Put one end of the rod into the bracket and place the other bracket in position. Install the other end of the rod and mounting screws in the bracket and tighten them. Then go back and tighten the first set.

Materials, Supplies, Tools

shower rod
mounting hardware
plastic anchors
masking tape
hammer
nailset
electric drill
carbide-tipped drill bit
measuring tape
screwdriver

Project 29

Make a Rag Bath Mat

Our homespun bathroom mat is so easy to make that everyone in the family can take part in the production. Choose a selection of fabrics to coordinate with a color scheme or create a one-of-a-kind mat using miscellaneous fabric scraps. If you sew, there are probably enough remnants in your basket to make several of these handy mats, which can be used anywhere in the house.

This is a project for one of those foul weather weekends when you want to stay indoors. You can listen to CDs all afternoon or "veg out" in front of tube—this is a project custom-made for couch potatoes. Sit comfortably stitching the mat as a laptop project or spread it out on top of a table or kitchen counter.

GETTING READY

You will need standard rug canvas with 3.3 holes per inch that is sold by the yard in craft stores. Our canvas bath mat measure 15 inches by 23 inches and requires enough scraps of fabric to equal 5 yards of 44-inch-wide material. The scraps of material are cut into 1-inch strips. You also need a blunt tapestry needle to stitch the strips through the holes in the canvas and iron-on rug binding that's sold in the notions department of a sewing store. It's approximately $1\frac{1}{2}$ inches wide and is ironed to the back surface of the mat.

Prepare the rug canvas by trimming it to size.

Use masking tape to bind the edges of all four sides. Lay down a strip of tape sticky side up and place the edge of your canvas in the center of the tape. Then fold the tape over the edge of the canvas, sealing the tape against itself. Do this to all four sides of the canvas.

If the fabric you're using is new, run it through a wash cycle in the washing machine and dry it in the clothes dryer to remove the sizing and make it softer and easier to thread in and out of the canvas holes.

Cut the material into 1-inch strips in various shades and patterns of fabric. Don't spend a lot of time being precise cutting the strips because the edges of fabric are not seen. You can save time cutting the strips by folding the fabric in half and cut through two thicknesses at one time. If you have (or can borrow) a rotary fabric cutter or pinking shears to cut the fabric, use them. They're faster than scissors and there's less fraying of the threads.

HERE'S HOW

The mat we made has 57 holes running vertically and 87 horizontally. It takes two strips of 44-inch-wide fabric to make one horizontal row. If your fabric is less than 44 inches wide or your mat is larger, you will need three or more strips per row.

You need to know only one simple stitch

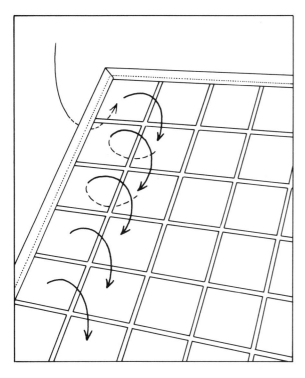

Using 1-inch strips of fabric, stitch on a diagonal, working from a hole in the bottom row to the next open hole that is above and diagonal to the last hole worked.

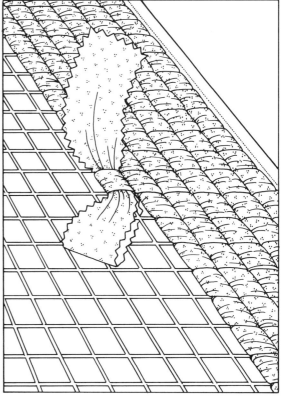

On the back side of the mat, tie off the end of a strip by slipping it under the last stitch. Then begin a new strip by securing it under the second-to-last stitch, which is on the left of the last stitch.

called the continental stitch. Thread the needle with a strip of fabric. Begin the first horizontal row in the lower left-hand corner of the canvas. Pull the threaded needle up through the first corner hole. Work from left to right across the canvas. Push the needle down through the hole that is diagonally adjacent to, or in the row above, it. Then pull the needle up through the hole directly below it. Continue across the width of the canvas repeating this stitch. The stitch slants to the right and covers two rows of holes.

When you have about 6 inches of fabric remaining it's time to splice on another strip of fabric. First you secure the short end under the last stitch. Push the needle through the canvas and then turn it over. Pull the needle until the fabric is tight, then slip the needle underneath the last stitch and pull it back toward the left to tighten the stitch on itself. Pull the strip tight and then cut it off with about a 1-inch tail end.

Start the new fabric strip on the backside of the canvas by pushing the needle through the second-to-last stitch and then up through the next open hole. Turn the canvas over and continue sewing the fabric strip into the canvas. At the end of the row, turn the canvas to its backside and secure the last stitch, such as you did in the middle by pulling it over itself.

Continue stitching the next row just as you did the first one and work your way across the mat. The fabric strips shred sometimes so just snip off the loose threads as you go along. Also cut off any threads dangling off the face of the mat.

When all stitching is completed remove the masking tape around the edges and attach iron-on rug binding to conceal the rough edges and finish the mat. Cut four pieces of binding, two for the long side and two for the short. Make each about two inches longer than necessary.

Turn the mat over so the back is up. Begin at one long side and fold back the edge of canvas that is not filled with fabric strips. (It used to have tape covering it.) Press the canvas flat and then lay on a strip of binding tape and iron it in place. Do this to the other sides.

The mat might become misshapen while you're working on it. If that's the case you can reshape it by blocking it back to the correct shape. To block the mat pin it down on the back of a larger throw rug of some other soft surface. Turn the mat face side down and use straight or T-pins to secure it in position, making certain that the corners are square and the edges are straight. Use a spray bottle to lightly mist the back of the mat with water and then spread a damp towel over it. Remove the towel and let the mat dry naturally to its correct shape.

Materials, Supplies, Tools

16 × 24-inch rug canvas (3.3 holes per inch)
44-inch-wide fabric to equal 5 yards
iron-on rug binding
straight or T-pins
scissors
masking tape
clothes iron
blocking board or rug
tapestry needle
measuring tape
spray bottle
damp towel

CHAPTER FIVE

Doable Door
and
Ceiling Projects

Project 30

Install a Lever Door Handle

Lever door handles are on the list of options from many new home builders because their sleek new look is a distinct improvement over the ordinary round knob. We think the best reason for a lever handle is more practical. If you've ever been laid up with a wrist or arm injury, you know how difficult it is to open a door equipped with a traditional round knob. Gripping and twisting the knob is very difficult and sometimes downright impossible. A lever handle is easy to open because it requires only a downward push.

Replacing a latch with a door knob on an interior door with one equipped with a lever handle is a job most anyone can complete in an hour. The reason this job is so simple is because you can make a one-for-one swap.

GETTING READY

Before you go shopping for a replacement latch with a lever handle, take a good look at the latch you want to replace. Most interior doors have tubular or cylinder type locks. This type of lock usually has round trim rings called "roses" around the door knob and a single latch plate held in place with a couple of screws mounted in the edge of the door.

All new door handles are designed for do-it-yourself installation so they come with complete directions from the manufacturer. Before you do anything, read the instructions. The first steps will deal with drilling holes for the lockset. (Skip this section in the directions because the holes are already in your door.) The installation instructions give you a good idea about how the old lock comes out, since it is generally the reverse procedure as the installation.

If you have a really old house, your doors might have a mortised or flush mounted latch. We don't recommend that you attempt to replace your mortise locks because they are set into the edge of the door and require considerable carpentry work to replace. Flush mount locksets are also more difficult to replace since you have to drill several large-diameter holes for the new lock in the door.

HERE'S HOW

Before you can install the new lockset you must remove the old one. Begin by removing the door knobs. Most have a set screw in their shaft. Just loosen the screw and unscrew the knob. Others have a small slot in their shaft. Insert the tip of a screwdriver in this slot and then, as you remove the screwdriver from the slot, pull the knob off the shaft.

Next, remove the rose trim pieces. Some are held in place with a couple of screws, others snap over a base plate. If you see some screws in the face of the plate, loosen them, and the round

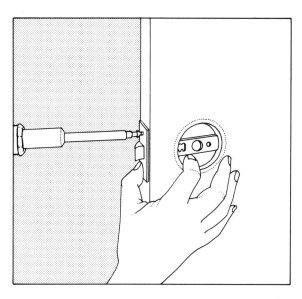

After removing the old lockset install the new latch bolt assembly into the old hole. Tighten the mounting screws until they are just snug enough to allow for final alignment.

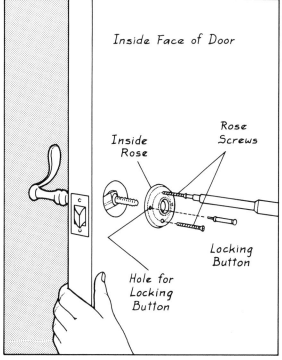

Inside Face of Door

Rose
Screws

Inside
Rose

Locking
Button

Hole for
Locking
Button

The rose/lever assembly is held in place by two screws. Push the lever, rose, and lever shaft through the center of the latch hub and then tighten the screws.

plate will come loose. If not, insert the blade of your screwdriver under the rose ring and pop it off the base plate. Then remove the screws from the mounting plate.

With the roses and/or base plates loosened you can remove the lock cylinder by pulling it straight out of the door. Some will come out from only one side, other types can be removed from either side.

When the cylinder is out loosen the mounting screws in the face plate of the latch assembly (which is in the edge of the door) and pull it straight out. Now you're ready to install the new latch.

Installing the new latch is easier than trying to figure out how to get the old one out. The only problem you may encounter is if the latch plate mounting screws are in a slightly different location than the old ones. If this is the case, just dip the shaft of a wooden match into some glue and push it into the old screw holes and then break it off flush with the edge of the door. Push in as many matches as possible to completely fill the holes and allow the glue to dry. With the holes filled new ones can be made next to the old ones.

Place the new latch plate into the edge of the door and then insert the knob assembly through the hole in the latch hub. The shaft of the knob is square so you have to align it with the square hub hole.

The two halves of the knob assembly are held together with two screws. One rose has holes in it for these screws, the other has threaded screw posts to accept the screws. Place the rose with the screw holes on the inside side of the door. Put the other rose on the other side of the door, align the holes with the screw posts, insert the screws, and assemble the lock. Tighten the screws but leave them loose so you can make slight adjustments for best alignment.

Install the levers on the protruding shafts and then check for free movement. If the lever is hard to turn or the latch does not snap open when the lever is released, wiggle the assembly to help establish proper alignment. Then tighten the screws in the face of the latch and in the rose.

The latch bolt should fit into the old striker plate so you can leave it in place. Chances are, you will want to remove the old one and install the new plate so it matches the lockset.

Materials, Supplies, Tools

lever door handle
wooden matches
wood glue
screwdriver (blade type and possibly Philips)

Project 31

Install a Pet Door

Our smoky gray cats—Pete and Repeat—use the great outdoors more than their litter box, but we still keep one on hand. Before we installed a pet door leading from the kitchen to the utility room (which isn't heated or used often), the box was a nuisance to keep underfoot. The pet door allows the Pete Brothers access to their litter box without leaving a door open to an unheated space, no small concern in our energy-conscious household. These doors are a nice addition to any household where the needs and wants of the family pet are as important as those of its other members.

A pet door consists of a metal frame that surrounds a rubber flap or door that a pet can push through to get to the other side. There's also a fiberboard door that can be secured in place if you want to confine the pet to either of the areas.

We considered installing a pet door so Pete and Repeat could go outside, but two things changed our mind. First, we didn't want them outside overnight; and second, we didn't want unannounced visits from other animals.

Installing one of these small doors within an interior door is an afternoon project at best. Only a few tools are needed, and if your pet is at all curious (and whose isn't?) you'll have their companionship and supervision as you grope around on the floor at their level.

Pet doors are available in all good pet supply stores. They come in various sizes so choose a door that fits your animal. The openings range from a small rectangle like ours, which measures approximately five inches by eight inches to bruiser-size doors with openings for German shepherds and larger dogs. Some other likely places to install a pet door might be in a door leading to the garage, in a basement door, or in a door to the front or back porch. You'll find pet doors sold at pet and hardware stores and home centers.

GETTING READY

The easiest and best-looking installation is through a solid wood door. A hollow core door is easy to cut but the gap between the inner and outer skin of the door does not present a finished look to the installation. The solution to this problem is to mount the outside frame that has the flap attached to it on the side of the door that faces your living area. This hides the hollow core that is visible only when the flap is up and your pet is using the door. Before you begin the installation decide which side of the door should look best and then install the outside frame on that side.

97

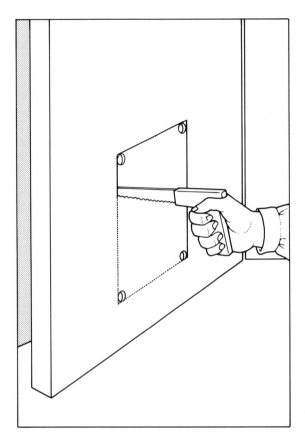

Trace the pet door opening on your door and then drill ¹/₂-inch holes in each corner. Cut from corner hole to corner hole with a keyhole saw and then remove the waste (cut-out) piece.

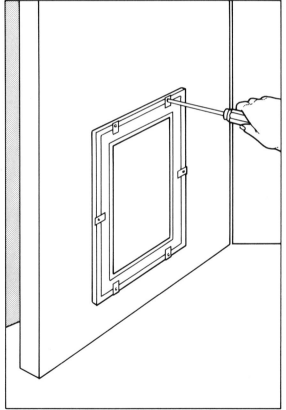

Both sides of the pet door have trim plates that are held in place with mounting screws. Install the frame with the flap on the side of the door facing your living area.

HERE'S HOW

Some doors come with a cutting template. Ours didn't, so we held the frame in position and used it as a template. Be sure to locate the door at least 2 inches from the bottom edge of the door so it doesn't interfere with the lower framing of the door, and position it at a convenient height so your pet can easily negotiate the opening. Before you do any cutting hold your pet next to the door outline and check the height of the door.

Use a pencil to trace around the inside of the frame or template and mark the location of the mounting screws. Drill a $1/2$-inch hole in each corner of the door outline. Use an inexpensive spade bit in your electric drill to make these holes. Then cut from hole to hole along the layout lines with a keyhole saw. Keep the saw cutting on the outside of the layout lines—that is, leave the pencil line on the waste part that will fall out.

Drill pilot holes for the mounting screws next. These holes must be straight or the screws will angle off and not be aligned with the frame on the other side of the door. Put the frame in posi-tion and use it as a template. Drill halfway through the door and then use the other frame as a template drilling from the other side. The holes should meet in the center. If they don't, work the drill up and down in the hole on both sides until they connect.

The door assembly goes quickly. Place the outside frame with the door in place on the dress side of the door and push the mounting screws through the template and into the door. Slip the other frame over the screws and thread on the washers and nuts. Check alignment and then tighten the screws.

Materials, Supplies, Tools

pet door (to fit your pet)
electric drill
$1/2$-inch spade bit
keyhole saw
screwdriver
scissors
measuring tape
pencil

Project 32

Install Space-Saving Bifold Doors

Unless space is at a premium, most of us don't question how a door operates and how much space it takes up. A standard door protrudes into a room when it's open and takes up room in the door jamb. The same is true for a sliding door, which allows full access to only half of the doorway opening at one time.

Most bifold doors give excellent access to your closets, laundry area, pantry, or whatever you want tucked behind them, but they still take up a lot of space in the room when they're open and protrude quite a bit into the door jamb.

We found bifold door hardware that gives you complete access to the area behind the doors. It's a hinge system that allows the door panels to remain folded flush against the walls, providing complete jamb-to-jamb access. It has an adjustment pivot bar that replaces the standard track to allow the inside door to swing out of the jamb.

We've used this arrangement in several houses to hide a built-in desk area, a place for fitness gear, and a sewing center. This hardware teamed with bifold doors creates many possibilities for using closet or alcove space.

GETTING READY

The size of the door jamb will determine the number of bifold door panels that you need. Two bifold doors can be used in openings up to 36 inches; anything larger and a four door system is usually preferred. The individual doors are smaller and fold into a more compact sandwich against the wall.

Bifold doors are available in sizes to fit just about any standard opening. If you require a four door setup, purchase two sets of hardware.

HERE'S HOW

To replace a standard door with a set of bifold doors or change the hardware on existing doors so they can open fully requires more thinking and planning time than it does actual work. The hinges are self-aligning, so most of the clearance dimensions between the doors is maintained by the hinge design.

The first step in this project is to mount the hinges on the door jamb and one of the bifold doors. Begin at the door jamb and install the pin side of the hinge. Measure $7\frac{1}{8}$ inches down from the top of the jamb and mark the edge of the jamb. Make a second layout mark at 69 inches down from the top of the jamb. Install a hinge pin up at each of these marks. Align the hinge so the top edge of the hinge is on the layout line with the front of the hinge flush with the casing.

On the hinge side of the bifold door make layout lines 7 inches and 69 inches down from the top of the door. Install the other half of the hinge

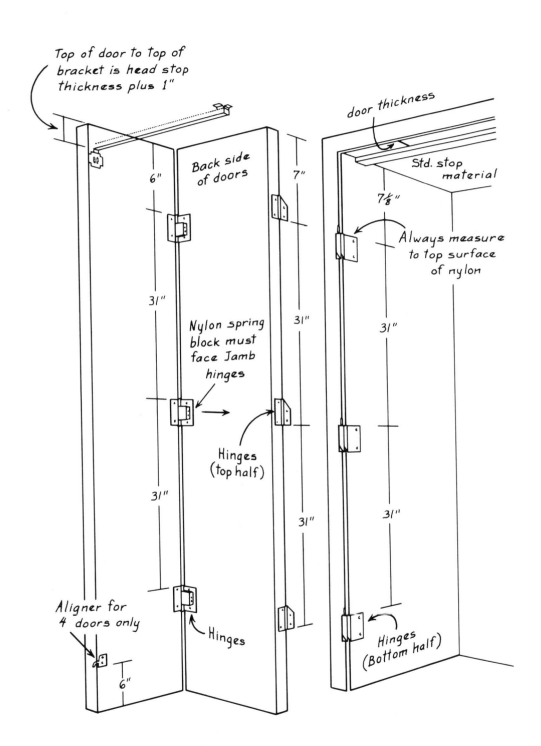

Top of door to top of bracket is head stop thickness plus 1"

Back side of doors

6"

7"

door thickness

Std. stop material

7⅛"

Always measure to top surface of nylon

31"

Nylon spring block must face Jamb hinges

31"

31"

Hinges (top half)

Hinges

31"

31"

31"

Aligner for 4 doors only

6"

Hinges

Hinges (Bottom half)

101

Replace a standard closet door with a bifold door and special hinge hardware to gain full use of a closet. These doors fold flat against the wall instead of taking up room inside the door jamb.

so the hole is facing down and its bottom edge is aligned with the layout mark and flush against the face of the door. Hang the door and test its fit. Install the hinges on the other jamb side door if you are hanging four doors.

Remove the door from the jamb hinges. Join it with the other doors with the hinges provided. Place the doors face side down and then carefully align the doors at the top and bottom. Locate the door hinges 6 inches from the top of the doors and then on 31-inch centers. To install, open the hinges and place them on the doors in alignment with the layout lines. Check that the locating flanges are tight against the jamb side door (the door with hanging hinges) and then use each hinge as a template to mark the location of the pilot holes with a pencil. Drill $1/8$-inch pilot holes for all screws and fasten the hinge to the doors with the hardware provided. Rehang the doors and check their movement.

The last step is to install the control arm. Check to see if your jamb has a door stop, which is a strip of wood running down the center of the jamb that prevents the door from moving completely through the jamb. If there is one, measure its thickness and add 1 inch to the measurement to calculate how far down from the top of the door to mount the control arm bracket. Install the bracket on the back of the outer bifold door so that it is flush with the edge of the door and the proper distance down from the top. Adjust the length of the control arm so that it's $1/4$ inch less than the width of one door. Attach the arm to this bracket and then open the doors so they lie flush against the wall. Screw the other end of the bracket to the jamb center or to the stop, and the door is ready to use.

If you are installing new doors, it is much easier to apply the finish before mounting the hardware on it. When the finish is dry install the hardware and put them in position.

Materials, Supplies, Tools

bifold doors
folding door hardware set
measuring tape
electric drill
drill bits
screwdriver
pencil

Source

Johnson Series 1601 Folding Door Hardware Set
L. E. Johnson Products, Inc.
P.O. Box 1126
Elkhart, IN 46515

Project 33

Replace Acoustical Tile with Tin Ceiling Panels

Here's the easiest way ever to distinguish a room with an authentic tin ceiling. Using an existing grid ceiling system, you can replace ho-hum acoustical tiles with authentic pressed tin ceiling panels. The key to this transformation is painting the grid system to match the color of the tin ceiling panels, which creates an even, unbroken appearance—one that looks much like a charming original.

The 24-inch square tin panels come in various stamped 30 gauge steel decorative patterns and designs reminiscent of the late nineteenth century. These new square panels make it possible to drop them in any grid ceiling system. Use an oil-based (alkyd) paint to paint both the grid and tin panels. The project is an easy weekend affair with considerable drying time needed for the grid and panels.

GETTING READY

Lay down old sheets or drop cloths to protect the floor below the ceiling. Remove the existing acoustical tiles from the grid system by pushing up on each one in its center. Tilt one side of a tile up so that its other side can be lowered down through the opening. Remove all the tiles in this way. Then use the crevice tool of a vacuum cleaner to remove dust from inside the channels of the metal grid. Next remove dust that's accumulated

around all the corners and crannies of the grid.

Wipe liquid deglosser on a rag and use it on the grid to remove dirt and grease before priming and painting. It dries quickly so the grid can be painted immediately.

HERE'S HOW

If there are rusty areas on the grid, use a wire brush to remove loose and chipped paint, then sand the rough areas smooth. Paint the grid with a metal primer and let it dry thoroughly. A foam applicator works well for this job. When it's dried, use an oil base paint with a narrow bristle brush to paint the grid. Take care to brush on the paint so that it's even and smooth, stroking the brush along the length of grid parts—not across them—for best results.

While the grid is drying, paint the tin ceiling panels with the same alkyd paint, using a wider bristle brush. Apply the paint to the panels by first brushing the paint in one direction, then go back with your brush spreading it in the other direction. This two-direction application assures you that the paint will flow into the grooves and pattern of the panels. Don't apply the paint so thickly that it starts to fill in the grooves and intricate patterns.

Let the ceiling panels dry thoroughly. The longer you allow the paint to dry the better, so it

Tin ceiling panels transform a room with ordinary acoustical ceiling tiles into one with charming turn-of-the-century appeal. Paint the grid and panels the same color so it looks like one continuous material.

can cure and become hard and more scratch resistant. Then install the panels in the grid. Just lift each panel up, tilt it to one side, and push it through the grid. Then lower it into position.

Source

Shanker Industries, Inc.
P.O. Box 3116
Secaucus, NJ 07097
(201) 865-5990

Materials, Supplies, Tools

liquid deglosser
1 quart metal primer paint
1 gallon alkyd paint
rags
drop cloth
sandpaper
wire brush
foam applicator
1½-inch bristle brush
2½-inch bristle brush
tin ceiling panels

Replace a Lock Handle on a Screen Door

In many houses the hardest working door is the aluminum storm and screen door that leads to the kitchen or back door entrance. Wherever it's located it gets a workout. Frequently the door stands tough, providing years of service, but its handle breaks from continued stress and strain. Instead of replacing the standard push-type handle with another one, consider replacing it with a locking latch and door knob.

A door knob doesn't have the tendency to break off, and if it's equipped with a keyed lock you can keep the back door open with the screen door locked to enjoy the breeze and still be able to open the door from the outside. Everyone has at one time or another stood at a locked screen door and had to shout in for someone to open it. With this type of lock all you need is the key.

You'll find a good selection of replacement locking door knobs for an aluminum storm door sold in home centers and hardware stores. They cost about fifteen dollars and require only a few hours of work to install.

GETTING READY

Remove the old handle and take it with you when you shop for the replacement. Compare the replacement with the one you have and try to purchase a model that has the same mounting hole pattern. If you can't find a match, it's not a prob-lem. Drilling new mounting holes in the soft aluminum is not difficult, and all replacement latches come with installation templates to guide you.

Before you reinstall a new latch clean the area behind the handle, which is usually one of the dirtiest and most difficult to clean areas on the door.

HERE'S HOW

The unit we installed required three $1/2$-inch mounting holes. Two of the holes aligned with the old mounting holes, so we only had to drill one hole. Use the template supplied by the manufacturer to accurately cut out the mounting holes in the locations specified.

Align as many of the holes in the template with the existing holes and then tape it to the door. Drill new mounting holes where needed. To do this just drill through the paper or cardboard template into the door. The door is hollow so you will drill through one side first. Keep your drill level, especially when you start drilling into the other side of the door, to make certain that the holes will be aligned. Wear safety glasses to protect your eyes.

Remove the template and assemble the lock according to the manufacturer's directions. When both halves of the assembly are in alignment and the handle turns freely and the lock system works, tighten the mounting screws. Close the door and

Use the template as a guide for drilling mounting holes for the lock. Tape the template to the door and drill holes through the template and door where they're specified.

The lock is held in place with two screws. Place the outer half of the assembly on the door frame and then align the inside half so the screws will thread into the outside half. Tighten screws to secure the lock.

check the clearance between the inside latching handle and the old latch bar.

Most of the time the old latch bar can be used, but the lock comes with a new one, so why not use it? Remove the screws and replace the old lock with the new one. Before you tighten the screws open and close the door several times and check that the latch and bar operate properly. The mounting screws are in slots in the latch so you can move it up and down to achieve the best alignment.

The new lock allows you to lock the door from the inside but still be able to open the door with a key from the outside. It's a good idea to get a set of extra keys for all members of the family.

Materials, Supplies, Tools

replacement door knob
electric drill
drill bits
screwdriver
marker
masking tape
safety glasses

More-Room-
Than-You-Thought
Projects

Project 35

Build a Back-of-the-Door Storage Rack

Does anyone ever have enough storage space? We certainly don't. We designed this back-of-the-door storage rack for small stuff. It's ideal for the inside door of a kitchen pantry to hold canned goods and small food items or in a linen closet for medicine and bathroom supplies.

The storage rack doesn't have to go on a door, actually; it can be hung on any wall where you want to get organized and know what supplies you have. Try it in a garage for assembling small gardening and lawn items or in the basement or workshop to hold all the little miscellaneous items that accumulate in a typical household.

If you plan to hang the rack on the back of a door, check for clearance between door and inside shelves. If you have a long wall (and lots of stuff), you might consider making two or more of these racks and adjusting the dimensions slightly to fit your needs.

You can leave the unit unfinished or finish it off with a coat of semigloss oil base paint.

GETTING READY

This storage rack has only four different-size parts. It is easy to put together, and since it is meant to be painted and then hung on the back of a door, the joinery is not critical. Economy grades of wood work fine, but just make sure that all of the pieces are straight and without twists.

The major work in making this storage unit is cutting the sides and shelves to length. To save some money the back is made in two parts. This way you can cut it out of a half sheet of plywood and have little waste. If your lumberyard stocks quarter sheets of plywood, purchase two of them because they're easier to transport.

HERE'S HOW

Cut one 60-inch-long side and two 16-inch-long shelves from one of the 8-foot 1×4 pine boards. Cut the other side and two shelves from another 1×4 board. Cut the remaining three shelves from the third 1×4 board. Try to cut as accurately as possible when making the shelves, because if they are different lengths the assembly will be difficult. From the scrap cut $6\frac{1}{4}$-inch- and $9\frac{1}{4}$-inch-long pieces to act as spacers during final assembly.

Lay the sides next to each another and align them at the top and bottom. Lay out the nailing guidelines starting at the top. Measure $\frac{3}{8}$ inch down from the top and use a combination square and pencil to draw a straight line across both sides. From that line measure down 7 inches and draw another layout line. Measure 10 inches down from it and draw another layout line. Then repeat this three times. Measure up $\frac{3}{8}$ inch from the bottom and mark the last layout line on the pair of sides.

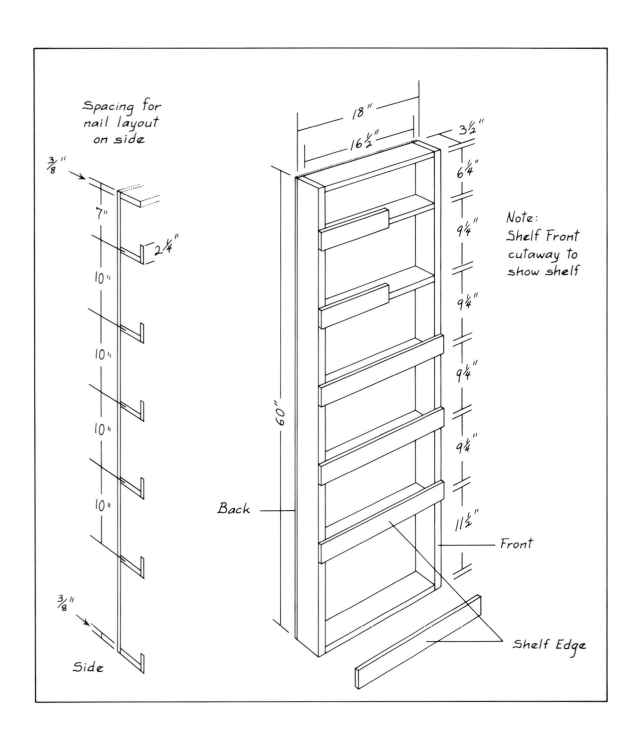

Spacing for
nail layout
on side

$\frac{3}{8}$ "

7"

2$\frac{1}{4}$"

10"

10"

10"

10"

$\frac{3}{8}$ "

Side

18"

16$\frac{1}{2}$"

3$\frac{1}{2}$"

6$\frac{1}{4}$"

9$\frac{1}{4}$"

9$\frac{1}{4}$"

9$\frac{1}{4}$"

9$\frac{1}{4}$"

11$\frac{1}{2}$"

60"

Back

Front

Note:
Shelf Front
cutaway to
show shelf

Shelf Edge

Drive three evenly spaced #6d finishing nails along the lines. Apply glue to the end of a shelf and nail the side to it, starting at the top. Place the 6 1/4-inch spacer on the side and butt it tight against the shelf you just installed. Butt the next shelf against the spacer, which will help hold the next shelf in alignment while you drive the nails through the side. Use the 9 1/4-inch spacer to install the next four shelves. Then install the bottom shelf flush with the end of the side.

Install the other side by applying glue to the ends of the shelves, and use the spacers to check the alignment of the shelves before you nail them in place. Then carefully place the side against the ends of the shelves. Don't slide it into position or you will smear glue over it. Start at the top and work your way down, nailing the side to the shelves.

Turn the unit facedown and use the combination square to check that the sides are square with the top and bottom shelves. Then apply glue to the back edge of the sides and shelves. Install the plywood back panels with #4d box nails spaced about eight inches apart around the perimeter.

Flip the unit over on its back and glue and nail the edges in place with 1-inch wire brads. Set the head of all finishing nails below the surface with a nailset and then fill in the depressions with wood filler. When the filler is hard, sand it smooth.

Paint the unit with several coats of a good-quality alkyd (oil-based) enamel. When it's dry it's ready to install on a door or wall.

Hanging the storage unit on a door is easy if you take the door off its hinges so you can work on it while it's horizontal. Place the storage unit on the door and position it so that it's centered. Then drill 1/8-inch pilot holes through the back into the door for the #8 mounting screws. Place two screws in the space between the top and first shelf and the bottom and the last shelf. Place another set in the center. Install the washers and screws and tighten them. Rehang the door and you are in business.

If you are going to hang the unit on a wall, use 2 1/2-inch-long #8 screws driven into the wall stud.

Materials, Supplies, Tools

3 8-foot 1 × 4 pine
12 linear feet of 2 1/4-inch pine lattice
half sheet 1/4-inch AC plywood
small box #6d finishing nails
small box #4d box nails
small box 1-inch wire brads
6 1-inch #8 round head wood screws and washers (for wall mounting, use 6 2 1/2-inch-long #8 screws)
small bottle carpenter's glue
3 sheets #120 grit abrasive paper
wood filler
1 quart paint
hammer
nailset
combination square
hand or circular saw
screwdriver
pencil
paintbrush

PARTS LIST			
NAME	AMOUNT	SIZE	MATERIAL
Side	2	$^3/_4'' \times 3^1/_2'' \times 60''$	pine
Shelf	7	$^3/_4'' \times 3^1/_2'' \times 16^1/_2''$	pine
Edge	7	$^1/_4'' \times 2^1/_4'' \times 18''$	pine lattice
Back	1	$^1/_4'' \times 18'' \times 60''$	plywood

Project 36

Line a Closet with Cedar

Most of us have a closet, probably in the extra bedroom, that is used to store off-season clothing. If you want to make it help protect the clothing, here's the perfect project for you. Line the walls of that closet with tongue and groove cedar boards or panels and create a moisture-resistant closet that helps prevent damage from moth larvae.

This project will take you the better part of a day. Much of the time you'll spend emptying the closet of its contents and removing the moldings along the floor. Cutting and installing the cedar panels is like assembling a jigsaw puzzle. The panels are tongued and grooved on the sides and edges so they fit snugly together. You secure them to the wall with construction adhesive.

GETTING READY

To determine how many square feet of cedar you'll need, measure the width and height of each wall and then multiply the numbers together to find the area. Multiply the length and width of the ceiling and add the wall and ceiling areas together to find the total amount of cedar you need. You get the most complete protection by covering all the surfaces in the closet with cedar, but if you're short on time do only the back wall or ceiling.

We found the easiest material to work with is 1/4-inch-thick tongue and groove cedar boards. These are sold in packages that cover about 10

square feet. Check the package for the exact amount of coverage. You'll need a tube of construction adhesive for each package of cedar lining you purchase.

Empty the closet of its contents and then remove the clothes rod and any shelving.

HERE'S HOW

This is a good woodworking project for first-timers, because your handiwork will be hidden away behind doors and clothes! If you make a mistake, you'll be the only one who knows about it. To get a neat, professional-looking job remove the baseboard molding and install it over the cedar paneling after it's on the wall. If you don't have the time to remove the molding, leave it in place. The cedar boards are thin and can be installed on the wall to butt up to the top of the molding.

If you decide to remove the baseboard, begin by removing the base shoe, which is the small rounded piece of molding against the floor. Push the blade of a putty knife behind the molding to protect the wood. Then use a screwdriver or small pry bar to work the molding out from the wall. Don't pry up on only one end. Work down the molding, gradually forcing it away and eventually off the wall. Use the same procedure to remove the larger piece of base molding attached to the wall.

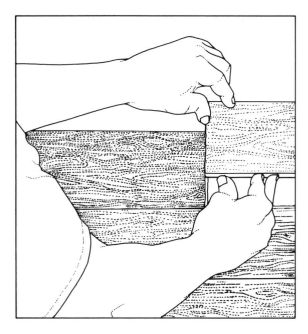

The cedar boards have interlocking tongue and groove edges. Check that you are cutting off the correct end when trimming a board to length.

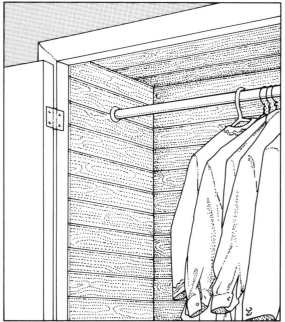

A closet lined in cedar protects clothing and linens from being damaged by moths.

Begin installing the cedar on the ceiling. Start the first row with the groove edge against the wall. The boards we used were 42 inches long. Each piece has a tongue and groove milled on opposite edges along its length. There is also a tongue and matching groove milled on opposing ends of these boards. These tongues and grooves allow the boards to interlock and provide a smooth surface. When you are cutting the boards carefully check to see which end you are cutting off. Once a board is cut only one end will have a tongue or groove. To get the most mileage out of your material start the next row with the cutoff piece from the previous row.

Cut off the tip of a tube of construction adhesive at a 45-degree angle to form a $\frac{1}{8}$-inch opening. Puncture the tube seal by inserting a piece of stiff wire, like a piece of coat hanger, through the tip opening and down into the tube. Once you feel the wire puncture the seal, place the tube in the caulk gun.

You can lay out the boards in any pattern that you choose. If you want to get fancy, lay out and install the boards on the diagonal, but you'll need extra boards and have to cut the starting and ending boards to a 45-degree angle.

To save yourself some cutting, install the boards parallel to the longest side of the ceiling. Lay out the first row and then cut the boards to length. Apply a long, skinny S-shaped bead of adhesive on the back of the board and place it in position on the ceiling. Then press it firmly in place. Finish off the row in the same manner. Cut and fit the next row of boards, apply adhesive, and install them. This cut procedure allows the adhesive to set up as you work.

The last row will probably have to be trimmed to fit. Cut the boards to length and then mark the side that should be cut away to remind you not to cut off the groove edge.

The procedure is the same for the walls. It's best to start on the back wall of the closet because it's usually the longest one. Then you can use up the short, cutoff pieces on the side walls.

After you are finished installing the paneling allow the adhesive to harden overnight before you reinstall the baseboard. Although the baseboard was originally nailed in place, another way to install it is using the same adhesive that you used to attach the cedar panels. Just use a few #6d finishing nails to hold the moldings in place while the adhesive sets. Don't glue the base shoe to the floor—apply adhesive only to the back of this molding.

Materials, Supplies, Tools

cedar panels
construction adhesive
#6d finishing nails
measuring tape
caulking gun
handsaw
hammer
putty knife
screwdriver

Project 37

Transform an Unfinished Attic into Storage Heaven

Unless you live in a twenty-room house, you're like most of us who are hard-pressed for storage space. If you have standing or crouching headroom in your attic, you can put it to work as a storage area. This project should take you a full weekend. Hauling the materials to the attic is no trivial task, so the job requires a strong back and stamina. We guarantee your newfound storage area will be well worth a few sore muscles.

Converting the unused space to usable storage involves laying down a subfloor of ⅝-inch-thick sheets of plywood on top of the existing ceiling joists. Since most unfinished attics are not designed to support a load, we suggest you also tie the floor joists to the roof rafters with some 1 × 4 lumber knee walls.

If you have only a small opening or hatch leading to the unused attic, consider hiring a carpenter to install a set of disappearing or pull-down stairs. Then you can follow up by finishing off the area for storage space as we describe here.

G E T T I N G   R E A D Y

Each 4 × 8-foot sheet of plywood covers 32 square feet of area. Unless the floor joists are at least 2 × 10 feet or larger, don't make the storage area wider than two sheets. You can run the plywood the full length of your attic. The plywood sheets should meet over a joist so all of its edges are supported. You might have to cut full sheets to fit. The joists are on 16- or 24-inch centers, so cutting should be minimized.

The easiest way to figure out a rough layout of the plywood is to cut a piece of scrap lumber to 8 feet in length and use it for a gauge. Take the board, a measuring tape, and a pad of paper and pencil to the attic.

The first thing to find out is if you can get an 8-foot-long board into the attic. If the full-length board won't fit, cut it down until you can maneuver it up and into the attic. This will determine the longest panel you can use in laying out the sheets of plywood. Remember that the plywood is 4 feet wide, so the panel must go straight up.

You should install the long side of the panels perpendicular to the direction of the joists, that is, the 4-foot edge should rest along and be supported by a joist. Use the board to help you determine the best sheet layout. Start by placing the end of the board at the opening and see where its far end falls. If it is not over a joist, adjust its position so it is. Move the board away from the opening until both of its ends rest on a joist. This might not be possible if you have cut the board down.

When both ends are supported on a joist you have found the location for the first full sheet. This should give you a good idea of how you have to cut the plywood so all panel joints fall over a joist. Work your way down the attic and keep count of

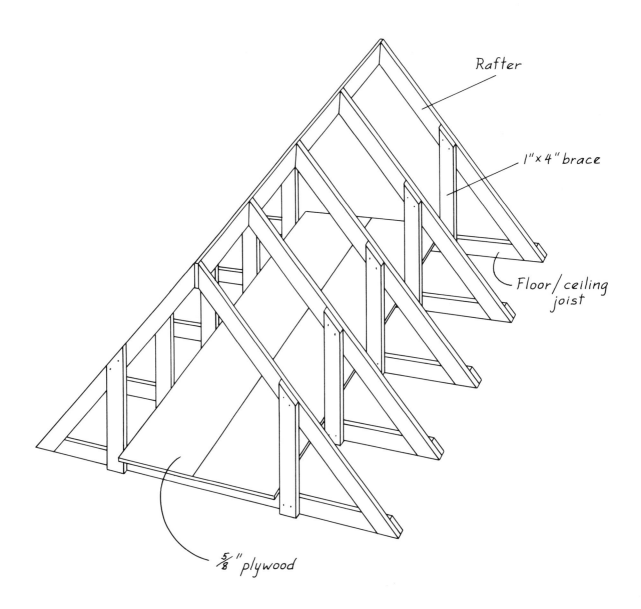

Rafter

1" x 4" brace

Floor/ceiling joist

$\frac{5}{8}$" plywood

Most attics provide usable storage if the ceiling joists are reinforced and a plywood floor installed.

the sheets as you go. When no more full sheets (or whatever the maximum length that will fit into the attic) are laid out, measure the distance from the edge of the last sheet. It should be over a joist, to the wall, or wherever you want to stop the floor. Cut a piece of plywood to this length from a full sheet. Count up the sheets. If you plan a double row to make it a deeper storage area, then double the number.

To find the length of the 1 × 4 braces to tie the floor joists to the roof rafters, estimate where the outer edge of the new floor will be and measure the distance between the ceiling joist that you are standing on straight up to the rafter. Add about a foot to the distance to calculate the length of the braces. Count the number of floor joists that you are covering with plywood and double the number to calculate the number of braces you need. Multiply the number of braces by their length and divide the number by 12 to calculate the number of feet of 1 × 4 stock to purchase.

Two people make this job go a lot faster and easier. If you don't have a van or vehicle to transport the load of 4 × 8 sheets of plywood and a pile of 1 × 4 braces, have the material delivered. Delivery charges are a lot less than the cost of new shocks for your car or repairing a dented roof.

HERE'S HOW

If you can't get a full sheet of plywood into the attic, rip (cut lengthwise) the plywood into 2-by-8-foot pieces. After you have figured the materials you need you should have a pretty good idea of the rough layout of the panels. They are held in place with #8d common nails.

Install the full-size panels first, but use only a few nails in the four corners and don't drive these all the way home or into the wood. Once you have the full-length panels in place and are sure that the ends fall midway on a ceiling joist, nail them in place. Place the nails about 10 inches apart.

Measure the length of the short panels and cut them to size. The easiest way to do this is to set the panels outside on the lawn on sawhorses. Mark the length of the panel at each side and then snap a chalk line between the marks. Cut along the chalk line.

Cut a test brace to use for a pattern to make all the braces you need. The test brace should be about 1 foot longer than the distance between the rafter and the floor joist. Take it to the attic and test its fit. If you have a steeply pitched roof, hold the board in position as plumb as possible, then mark the pitch of the roof on the end. Do this by sight—it does not have to be extremely accurate. Cut the end of the board to match the roof slope and then put the board back in position. Check that the board is tight or at least near the roofing sheeting. It should extend down beyond the floor joist at least 6 inches so it can be nailed to the joist. When you are satisfied with the fit of this test brace take it downstairs and cut the remaining pieces.

Nail the braces to the rafters and then to the joists with #8d common nails. To keep the rows of braces straight, install the end braces first and then stretch a chalk line between them at the rafters and snap a line. As you install the braces, butt the bottom against the plywood floor and align the top with the chalk mark on the rafter.

Materials, Supplies, Tools

4 × 8-foot sheets of $^5/_8$-inch plywood   chalk line

1 × 4 lumber   circular saw

#8d common nails   pencil

measuring tape   paper

hammer

Project 38

Build a Firewood Box

If you have a fireplace or wood-burning stove, you know about the warmth and charm that a glowing fire adds to a room. You know, too, just how messy the firewood can be. We've used straw baskets, brass buckets, and metal log carriers to hold firewood, but none of them have worked as easily and simply as a wooden box. We designed it open at the top so firewood can be dropped inside with a separate compartment for storing newspaper or kindling. It is 34 inches long, 22½ inches wide, and 17½ inches high so it can hold plenty of firewood.

Our slatted firewood box is like a crate, so it's easy to build and doesn't require much in the way of tools. It's designed around standard 1 × 4 and 2 × 2 lumber. We used a light oil finish to seal the wood and bring out the grain, but another option is to finish it with a wipe-on stain for a darker appearance. A painted finish isn't advisable because a load of heavy firewood dumped inside the box is likely to chip the paint.

G E T T I N G   R E A D Y

A firewood box isn't fine furniture; it's a utility piece, so just about any grade of lumber is suitable. It's a good idea to handpick the lumber so you get boards without loose knots. Also check to see that there are no knots along the edges of the boards, because they will be used full-width and the knotholes would be visible.

There are plenty of slats that need to be cut to length, so unless you have a circular saw, you may want to consider having the lumberyard cut the 1 × 4 stock to length. Give them the cutting list and you can haul home the cut slats for assembly.

H E R E ' S   H O W

Lay out the slats on the 1 × 4 stock, measure them, and then cut each piece to length. Don't take a shortcut and lay out several slats on the board and cut one after another, because the pieces will be short the thickness of your saw blade. Next cut the corner posts and end cleats to length from the 2 × 2 stock.

Begin assembly by laying the bottom slats next to one another on a flat surface. Next to them lay down the end cleats. In this step you will glue and nail the bottom parts to the end cleats. Pre-drive three nails into the ends of each of the bottom slats about ¾ inch from their ends. Apply glue to one of the bottom cleats. Then nail the first bottom slat to this cleat so the slat end is flush with the side of the cleat and the slat side is flush with the cleat end. Use your combination square to check that the slat is perpendicular to the cleat. Install the remaining five bottom slats in the same way and then glue and nail their other ends to the bottom cleat.

Assemble the ends of the firewood box in the same manner. Begin with the left end of the box.

Lay four ends on a flat surface and lay the corner posts next to them. The end and side slats are staggered to form a lap joint at the corners. To accomplish this, every other end slat is installed flush with the side of the corner post. Its other end extends beyond the post by ³/₄ inch. The slats are self-aligning. Just glue and nail the left end of the top side slat flush with the top and side of the end post. Place the other end post about ³/₄ inch in from the end of the side slat. But don't fasten it yet. Glue and nail the second side slat flush with the side of the end post. Check that it is snug against the top side slat and that the corner post remains flush with the top edge of the top side slat. Then go back and glue and nail the top side slat and the other end of the second side slat to the corner posts. Install the remaining slats by aligning them flush with the corner posts—the other end of each slat will fall into place.

Repeat the assembly sequence on the other end. Check that the offset of the side slats is exactly opposite that of the other end.

Glue and nail the end assemblies to the bottom. Drive the nails through the side slats about 1

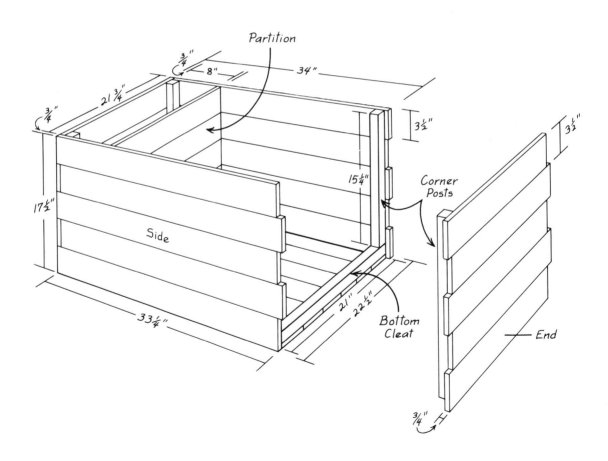

124

inch up from the bottom of the lower slat. Before you glue and nail the side slats in place turn the box on its side and check that the side assemblies are perpendicular to the bottom. Drive the nails through the side slats about 1 inch in from their ends so the nails penetrate into the corner posts.

When the sides are in place turn the box on its side so you can install the partition slats. To help keep the partition slats in alignment as you nail them in place, tack a piece of scrap 1 × 4 stock to the side of the box so its edge is 8 inches from one end and parallel to the end. Install another piece of scrap on the opposite side. Begin with the bottom partition slat and nail it in place, then install the next one.

Allow the glue to dry and then sand the firewood box lightly before applying a finish. We used an easy-to-apply natural color wipe-on oil finish.

Materials, Supplies, Tools

8 1 × 4 10-foot pine
2 2 × 2 10-foot pine
carpenter's glue
small box #6d finishing nails
wipe-on oil finish
hammer
measuring tape
combination square
hand or circular saw
rags
sandpaper

PARTS LIST

NAME	AMOUNT	SIZE	MATERIAL
Bottom slat	6	$3/4'' \times 3^1/2'' \times 32^1/2''$	pine
Side slat	10	$3/4'' \times 3^1/2'' \times 33^1/4''$	pine
End slat	10	$3/4'' \times 3^1/2'' \times 21^3/4''$	pine
Partition	4	$3/4'' \times 3^1/2'' \times 21''$	pine
Corner post	6	$1^1/2'' \times 1^1/2'' \times 15^1/4''$	pine
End cleat	2	$1^1/2'' \times 1^1/2'' \times 21''$	pine

CHAPTER SEVEN

Energy-Saving Ideas

Project 39

Make an Interior Storm Window

To control condensation and air infiltration in windows, you have a choice: pay a carpenter about $250 to replace the window for a better insulated one or purchase a dehumidifier that costs upward of $100. A much less expensive solution is to make your own interior storm window. This simple window will solve or significantly help reduce condensation, which damages interior woodwork and leaves nasty water stains on curtains and draperies. It also helps lower your energy costs by tightening up drafty windows.

The frame for the storm window is made of aluminum screen channel and corner brackets, which are sold for making replacement screen panels. It is available in white or aluminum finish and sold in 10-foot lengths at most hardware stores and home centers. We used 4-mil plastic sheeting for glazing these frames instead of screen fabric. These inexpensive components allow you to quickly build a custom interior storm window.

GETTING READY

To determine the exact size of the interior storm window requires carefully measuring the window recess. The bottom of the frame will rest on the windowsill and its top and sides must touch the window jamb.

If your window has protruding hardware like opening cranks or locking levers, you may be better off attaching the storm windows to the window casing. If there are shades or blinds in the window jamb, you may have to remove them, install the storm window tight against the window sashes, and then reinstall the shade or blind.

To make a storm window that fits inside the window jamb measure the jamb height at each side of the window. These may be different if the window jamb has bottomed out of plumb through the years. Measure the jamb width at the top and bottom because they may be different, too.

To build a storm window that is installed on the casing, make the storm window larger than the size of the window jamb. If your windows are framed with fancy moldings, check that the storm window you plan to make will rest on a flat part of the molding.

You need to purchase enough aluminum screen channel, rubber spline, and foam weather stripping to reach around the perimeter of your window, plus an additional foot. Plastic sheeting is sold in various widths from 3 feet to 8 feet wide. Purchase enough sheeting so it will overlap the finished frame by 3 to 4 inches.

You can push the rubber spline into the groove in the aluminum screen channel with a screwdriver, but it is a lot easier to do with a spline roller, also called a screen and glass installation tool. This inexpensive tool (three dollars or less) looks like a pizza cutter and is used to force the spline into the frame groove.

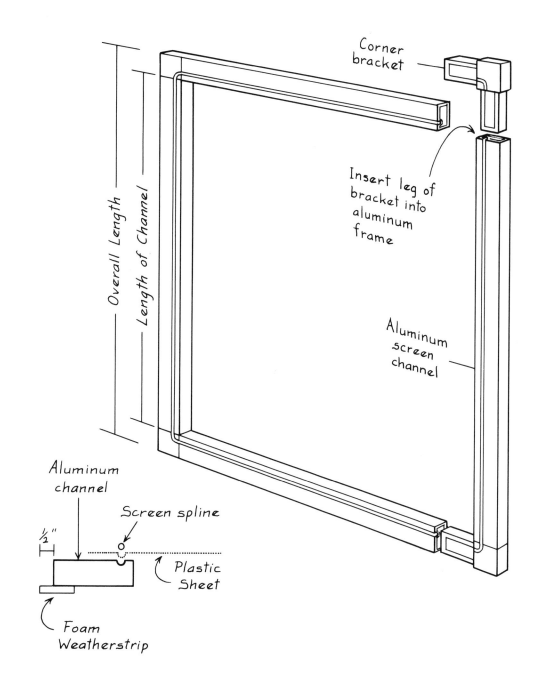

Corner bracket

Insert leg of bracket into aluminum frame

Aluminum screen channel

Overall Length

Length of Channel

Aluminum channel

Screen spline

½"

Plastic Sheet

Foam Weatherstrip

The same easy-to-assemble aluminum frame used to make a screen can also be used to construct an effective storm window.

129

HERE'S HOW

Constructing the frame is easy because the aluminum screen channel is designed to be connected together with special corner brackets. With these brackets you don't have to worry about making a miter cut at each corner.

Cut the aluminum screen channel to size with a hack saw equipped with a fine-toothed (32 teeth per inch) blade. Remember you must take into consideration the width of the four corner brackets when you cut these parts. For example, if the corner brackets are 1 inch wide, just the actual square part that forms the corner, not the legs, are inserted into the aluminum frame. Subtract 1 inch from the length of the frame for each corner bracket. The aluminum screen channel should be cut 2 inches shorter than the overall dimension of the storm window frame.

Lay out the four pieces to form the shape of the window and insert the plastic corner brackets into the aluminum frame members. You might have to file the inside of the aluminum frame to remove any burrs or rough areas that prevent the legs of the corner bracket from fitting into the frames.

Test fit the frame into the window jamb. You should have a snug fit on all sides. The aluminum is easy to cut, so you can go back and trim one of the sides if it's too long. Adjust the fit of the frame so there are no large gaps between it and the jamb.

Cut the plastic sheeting at least 3 inches larger than the frame size. Then lay it on the frame so it overlaps on all four sides.

Begin inserting the rubber spline in one corner. Press the end of the spline into the groove with the tip of the spline roller. Work your way up the sides of the frame pressing the spline into the groove. At the corners work the spline around the corner and then start down the next side. As you work around the perimeter, pull the plastic sheeting taut. Don't try to stretch it tight—just keep it wrinkle free. As the spline is pushed into the groove, it pulls the plastic tight. When you reach the last corner, trim the spline so it meets in the corner. Trim off the excess plastic sheeting with a sharp utility knife. Cut the plastic off as close to the spline as possible.

Install foam weather stripping on the back side (facing the glass side of the window) of the frame. Peel off the protective paper backing and stick the weather stripping to the frame so that $1/8$ inch of the foam strip overlaps the frame. As you look at the inside of the frame (facing the room), you should see weather stripping protrude $1/8$ inch past the edge of the frame on all sides.

Secure the new storm window in the frame by pushing it into the frame until it rests tight against the lower window sash. The tight fit of the weather stripping between the jamb and frame keep it in place while it seals off any small cracks.

If you are mounting the storm window on the casing, the weather stripping does not have to protrude past the frame.

Materials, Supplies, Tools

4-mil plastic sheeting
aluminum screen channel with corner brackets
1-inch-wide self-stick foam weather stripping
screen spline
hack saw

utility knife
measuring tape
file
splining tool

Project 40

Install a Setback Thermostat

The cost of heating or cooling a house is becoming a big ticket item in most everybody's budget. If you live in the South, your money is spent on air conditioning, and in the northern states keeping a house warm in the winter takes lots of energy dollars.

No matter where you live, one of the best ways to help you save energy and money is to install a setback thermostat. Now that's not exactly earth-shattering news for anybody. But what is newsworthy is the latest version of setback thermostats featuring multiple cycles. Older types of setbacks allowed for only one, or at best two cycle changes. You can set back the temperature to a money-saving lower setting during the evening hours while everyone is sleeping and then automatically raise the temperature in the morning.

Newer programmable thermostats allow for more complex cycles that allow you to raise or lower the heating or cooling setting on the thermostat to fit your life-style. A typical program might run like this: At 6:30 A.M. the heat rises from an energy-saving 55 degrees to 70 degrees for showering and breakfast. Everyone is on their way by 8:30 A.M., so the temperature is lowered to 65 until 11:30 A.M., when some family members show up for a lunch break and want it 70 degrees. The thermostat sets back the temperature down to 65 until 4:00 P.M., when people start returning home from school and work. The thermostat then maintains the temperature in the house at 70 degrees until 10:30 P.M., when everyone is ready for bed.

A different program can be set for each day of the week. The new thermostats can also be programmed for a separate cooling cycle. Of course you can override the program any time you want.

GETTING READY

Throughout the evolution of heating and cooling systems there have been many types of thermostat controls installed. When you pull your old thermostat off the wall you will probably find that it has two, three, or even five or more thin wires connected to it. The new setback thermostats are designed to work with most systems and come with specific easy-to-follow wiring diagrams.

Installing a thermostat is safe because most heat control devices run on 24-volt circuits. This low voltage does not present a shock hazard. Some systems, especially electric heat, use standard house 120-volt house current. If your thermostat is connected to thin wires coming directly out of a hole in the wall, then you have a safe 24-volt system. If the thermostat is connected to an electrical box, don't attempt to install a standard setback thermostat until you seek professional help.

Before you shop for a setback thermostat take a look at your old one. Remove the cover. Most of them snap off but some are held in place with a couple of screws. Look at the screw terminals and see how many wires are connected to them. If there are five or less, you will be able to make the swap yourself.

When shopping for a thermostat consider your present *and* future needs. If you don't have central air conditioning, then purchase a unit for heating only. But if you do plan to install air conditioning in the near future, consider this feature. The more features the thermostat has, the more expensive it is and the longer you will take to recover your investment. Don't skimp. If the thermostat can't handle your schedule, you might not be able to take full advantage of potential energy savings.

HERE'S HOW

Turn the power off to the furnace at the main switch or open the circuit breaker serving the furnace. If you haven't already removed the cover of your old thermostat, take it off. Before you remove any wires make a diagram of the position of each wire and what terminal it is connected to on the thermostat. Most replacement setback thermostats come with stick-on wire identification tags that make this process easy. It is very important that you identify each wire before you remove it. With a two-wire system it does not matter which wire is attached, but it does on a five-wire system and there are twenty-five possible combinations. If you miswire the thermostat, there is a possibility you will damage it.

After you have the wires identified, remove the old thermostat. You can sometimes detect how many layers of paint or wallpaper have been ap-

plied to the wall with the cover removed. Usually the new thermostat will cover up the wall area concealing mismatched paint or wallpaper discovered behind the cover. If the new thermostat is smaller than the old one, you may want to touch up this area with paint or wallpaper before you install the new thermostat.

The new thermostat will most likely be of the solid state type and be powered by a 9-volt transistor radio battery. Most of these do not use a mercury switch, so it's not important that they be mounted perfectly level. If you are installing one with a mechanical clock–type timer, you should take care to level this thermostat or you will not get accurate temperatures.

The thermostats come with mounting screws and wall anchors. Some manufacturers provide location templates, others direct you to use the base of the thermostat as a template. In either case, mark the location of the mounting screws on the wall and then drill a $3/16$-inch hole for each wall anchor. Tap the wall anchor into the hole and then install the mounting plate or body of the thermostat with the screws provided.

Wiring up the thermostat is not difficult; the only requirement is that you follow the directions exactly. The two-wire systems are very easy to wire. Most thermostats have a row of screw terminals. Connect either wire to the terminal marked with a W and the other wire to the terminal marked R. Loosen the screw, push the wire under the terminal arm, and then tighten the screw. Of course, if the specific installation directions provided by the manufacturer instruct you to connect these wires differently, follow those directions.

Other systems are just as straightforward to wire up, but because there are so many different

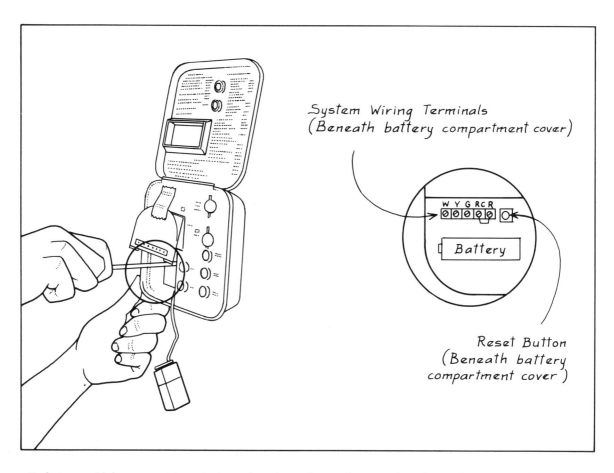

System Wiring Terminals
(Beneath battery compartment cover)

W Y G RCR

Battery

Reset Button
(Beneath battery
compartment cover)

Replacing an old thermostat with a setback type shown is easy because the terminals on the new thermostat are clearly marked. The 9-volt battery powers the thermostat's clock and computer.

possibilities you should follow the specific directions that come with the thermostat.

After the thermostat is wired install the 9-volt battery if one is required. Return the power to "On" to the furnace. Follow the directions in the owner's manual, which should tell you that you turn the thermostat on by placing it in either the "heat" or "cool" mode. Then put the thermostat into its "manual" mode and set the temperature a few degrees above the present room temperature, or lower it if you're testing the thermostat in the "cool" mode. If you experience any problems, refer to the trouble-shooting section of your owner's manual.

Materials, Supplies, Tools	Source
programmable thermostat	Magic Stat 7 Day Electronic Programmable
tape	Thermostat (Designer Model)
paper, pencil	Honeywell, Inc.
screwdriver	1985 Douglas Dr. North
hammer	Golden Valley, MN 55422-3992
wire cutter/stripper	
drill with bits	

Project 41

Disguise a Window Air Conditioner

Many of us have a window air conditioner that's semipermanently installed in a window. Ideally the unit would be removed from the window and stored for the winter, but often it's just too cumbersome to move or you don't have a place to store it.

For those units that are left in place during cold weather months it's a good idea to cover them for protection from the elements. This safeguard contributes to a longer running life for its parts and motor. A cover also stops chilly drafts from blowing through the unit into the house.

You can purchase a fabric or plastic cover that provides protection from the elements but does little to prevent heat loss through the steel frame of the air conditioner. By using an insulated cover you can stop a good percentage of the heat lost both through air infiltration and convection through the frame.

We have tried several different types of covers and have found that rigid foam insulation (sold in most lumberyards and home centers) is an effective and easy-to-use material. There are several different types of foam insulation and any of them may be used. The biggest problem with this type of insulation is that it deteriorates in direct sunlight. The first covers we made lasted a few years and by then they got pretty ratty looking. We found that a better material to use is foil-faced insulation board designed to be used as wall sheeting. The foil face is weather resistant and protects the foam.

R-Max is one national brand, but there are others and any type works. The $1/2$-inch-thick board is the easiest size to work with. It can be cut easily with a utility knife and glued together with contact cement.

GETTING READY

Foil-faced sheeting boards are sold in 4×8-foot sheets. This is more than what's needed to cover an average-size air conditioner. The corners of the sheeting boards are easily damaged, so look in the "half price" or "as is" bin of materials. You might find a few beat-up pieces for next to nothing.

Every air conditioner has a slightly different size, so rather than give exact measurements we'll explain how to measure your air conditioner and then use the measurements so you can custom cut the panels.

If you cut the foil board carefully, you can fold it, eliminating a lot of joints. If storage of the cover is a problem, then assemble it with duct tape so when it's not in use you can take it apart by opening its folded joints and storing it flat.

While shopping pick up five or six feet of shock cord and a couple of hook end fittings. The elastic cord is sold by the foot in many large home centers, or you can get it already made up with hooks on the ends in prepackaged lengths. Purchase several long lengths.

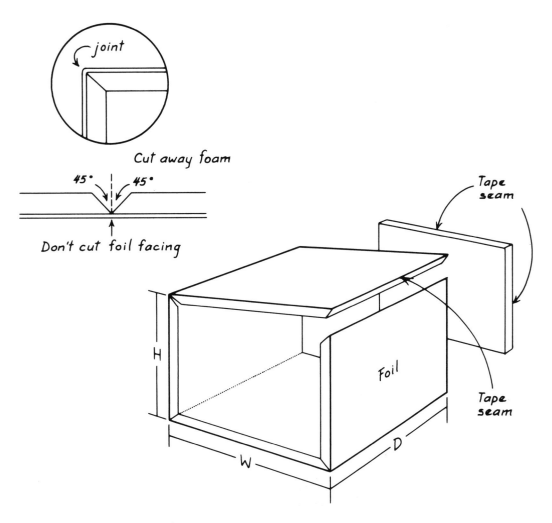

joint

Cut away foam

45° 45°

Don't cut foil facing

Tape seam

Foil

Tape seam

H

W

D

H = Height of Air Conditioner + 3"
W = Width of Air Conditioner + 3"
D = Depth of Air Conditioner + 3"

Measure the height, width, and depth of the air conditioner, add three inches to each measurement, then cut the insulation board as shown in the diagram.

HERE'S HOW

Standing at the air conditioner protruding out from the exterior of the house, run a tape measure from the farthest point and measure the depth that it sticks out. Then measure its height and width. Add three inches to all of these dimensions.

For example, one of our air conditioners measures 16 inches deep by 19 inches wide by 15 inches high. Add three inches to these measurements and you get D=19, W=22, and H=18. For an air conditioner this size you need one 19-by-22-inch top and bottom panel, two 18-by-19-inch side panels, and a back panel that measures 18 inches by 22 inches.

The easiest way to make the cover is to cut a piece of foam sheeting that is long enough to contain the two sides and the top and bottom panels. In our example, the piece should be at least 78 inches long. Then starting at one end mark the location of the different panels on the strip. Lay out the side, then the top, the other side, and finally the bottom.

At each of the layout lines remove a V-shaped wedge (see joint detail) of insulation but don't cut through the foil facing. This allows you to fold the panels into a box so you will only have to tape one joint together.

If you purchase scrap pieces of sheeting, cut the individual panels to size and tape all joints together.

Fold the joints to form right angle corners and tape the last joint together with duct tape. Cut the end panel to size and place it on one end of the box and tape it in place.

The easiest way to hold the cover in place is with a piece of shock cord. Install a screw eye in the window sash closest to the cover. Install another screw eye on the windowsill on the other side. To install the cover just slip it over your air conditioner and hold it in place with shock cord stretched from eye to eye. If you purchased a long piece of shock cord, make up a section with hooks on both ends. If you purchased prepackaged shock cords, hook several together and attach them from eye to eye to hold the cover in place.

Materials, Supplies, Tools

1 sheet R-Max or equivalent insulation board
  (4 × 8 foot)
6-foot shock cord
2 shock cord hook end fittings
1 roll 3-inch duct tape
1 small contact cement
utility knife
block of wood
2 screw-eye hooks
measuring tape

Install a Water Saver for Your Toilet

It's no secret that a toilet consumes a lot of water. By installing a simple water-saving device on a toilet used by a family of four, you can save a whopping 24,000 gallons of water a year. The newest water-saving device that we've found is called Future Flush, which is simple to install and goes a long way to conserve water.

The white plastic unit has a split handle that provides control of two flush cycles. The short flush lets an older toilet use a minimal amount of water for discharging liquid and paper waste. The longer handle controls a full flush cycle for positive flushing of solids. This device is easy to install and fits on 95 percent of existing toilets. You can choose from either a front- or side-handled toilet with a choice of white or chrome handles.

GETTING READY

This project involves replacing the guts of your toilet. It's basically a one-for-one swap because all the parts necessary are included in the kit. These parts are bolt-on or snap-on items, and the only tools you need are a screwdriver and an adjustable wrench.

Close the toilet seat so you don't drop one of the parts or a tool into the toilet bowl. Remove the tank lid carefully. Put it in a safe place outside of the bathroom so you don't damage it. (Remember that the water in the toilet tank is clean; the parts might be a little corroded or slimy, but there is little health hazard in reaching into the toilet tank.)

HERE'S HOW

Turn the toilet's water supply off at the shut-off valve below the toilet on the wall. Turn the valve handle clockwise. Then flush the toilet to empty the tank. There will be a little water in the bottom of the tank, so use a sponge to mop it up.

Since the parts have been in your toilet for a long time, removing the old flapper valve and flush arm assembly is probably harder than installing the new parts. Don't be alarmed if the screws or parts break when you attempt to remove them.

If you have a rod and ball valve, which is a large rubber ball screwed to the end of a rod, remove the rubber ball, rod, and guide by unclamping the guide from the overflow tube. Then unhook the rod from the flush arm and remove the assembly. A flapper-type valve is removed by twisting it off its mounting hooks or by slipping the mounting collar up and off the overflow tube.

The flush handle has a hollow threaded shaft that passes through the wall of the toilet tank. It is removed by loosening the large nut on the inside of the tank. You might need to use a wrench on this one but remember the threads are reversed so you loosen it by turning it counter-

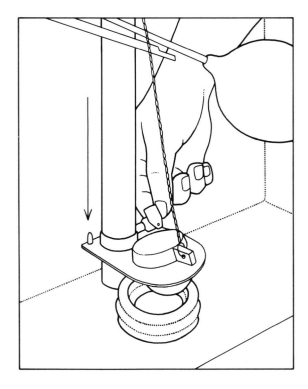

After removing the old flapper valve or flush ball and rod assembly, slip the new assembly down over the overflow tube.

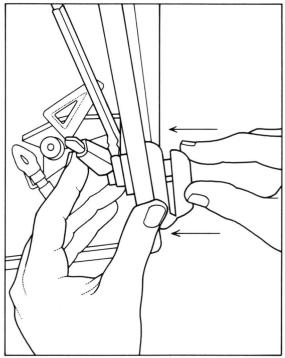

Replace the old flush handle with the new dual stage flush mechanism.

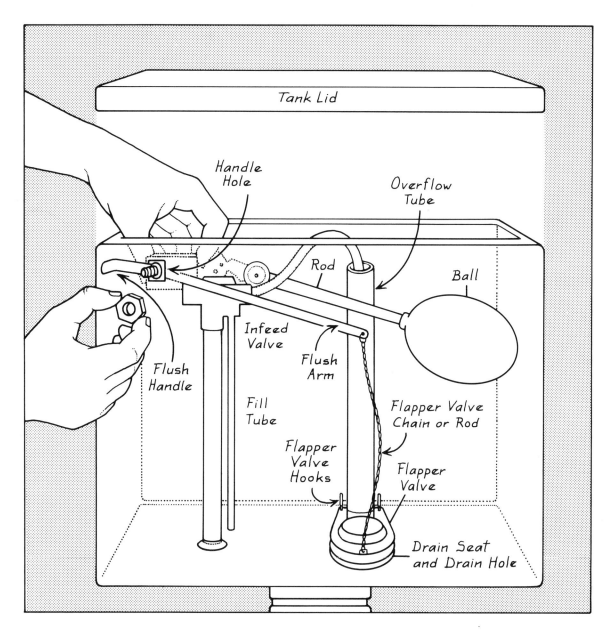

Tank Lid

Handle Hole

Overflow Tube

Rod

Ball

Infeed Valve

Flush Arm

Flush Handle

Fill Tube

Flapper Valve Chain or Rod

Flapper Valve Hooks

Flapper Valve

Drain Seat and Drain Hole

First install the long flush handle that controls the full flush cycle, then push the short handle on the shaft and tighten the setscrew.

clockwise as you look at the nut from the front of the toilet.

Install the new flush assembly. It goes in place exactly as the old one came out, but only the nut is on the outside of the toilet now. If the shaft is loose in the hole, use the adapter supplied with the new unit. Don't overtighten the nut—snug it up finger tight and then give it a turn with the wrench.

The flapper valve goes in next. If you had a ball and rod system, slide the mounting collar on the new flapper on to the overflow tube and push it down into position. If you had a flapper valve, chances are that you can install the new flapper on the old mounting collar. Then attach the beaded chain to the end of the flush arm and the flapper valve.

Once the adjustable flush mechanism and flapper valve are in place you have to fine tune the flushing mechanism to conserve the most water possible. There are full instructions included with the unit. The main adjustment is the positioning of the small float that is attached to the flush handle mechanism. Raise the float to lower water consumption in the short flush cycle.

Test the short flush cycle of your toilet by pressing the short handle. Adjust the float so the toilet uses the least possible water to clear the bowl of liquid and paper.

Materials, Supplies, Tools

Future Flush unit
screwdriver
adjustable wrench
sponge

Source

Future Flush, Con-Tech Industries
  104 South Mill
  Creswell, OR 97426
  (503) 895-3226

Project 43

Make a Sun Screen for a Patio Door

Most of us love a sunny day but a house with a southern exposure can suffer from constant direct sunlight. Paint takes a beating, but so do other parts of your house. Window screens are no exception. If made of steel, they eventually rust and if they are plastic the sun's UV (ultraviolet) light can shorten their service life considerably.

If you are faced with this situation, consider replacing the screening with SunScreen, a sun-resisting screen fabric that not only keeps pesky insects out but also reduces solar heat gain in the summer and heat loss in the winter. The screening also reduces glare and potential damage to drapes and furniture from strong sunlight. This material costs a few dollars more than standard fiberglass screening, but the vinyl-coated fiberglass screening resists shrinking and rotting. It comes in a variety of colors (grays, bronzes, and whites), so you can choose a shade that blends with the siding.

Replacing the screening in an aluminum storm window or door is easy. If you have ever sliced pizza with a pizza cutter, you can install screening.

G E T T I N G   R E A D Y

Screening comes in standard widths, so measure the width of your screen frame and purchase screening at least as wide and six inches longer than the height of the screen frame. You should also purchase a roll of rubber spline. The thin rubber tubing is sold by the foot or in packages. Get enough spline to go all the way around the perimeter of the screen frame plus about six inches.

We recommend that you purchase a spline tool, which is an inexpensive handle with a roller at each end. One roller is convex and is used to push the screen fabric into the groove in the frame. The other roller is concave and used to push the screen spline into the groove.

H E R E ' S   H O W

Remove the old screen by pulling the rubber spline out of its groove. If it's loose, simply grab one end of the spline and pull it out of the groove that runs around the frame. If it's tight, use a screwdriver to pry the end out of the groove, then grab the end with a pair of pliers and pull it loose.

Dust off any dried dirt from the frame and then clean it with a metal polish cleaner. (It'll look as if it's brand new.) Lay the frame down on a flat surface and spread the SunScreen material on top of the frame. Position the fabric so there's an equal amount of material on all four sides.

You don't have to crimp fiberglass screen with the convex side of the spline roller, so start installing the spline. Starting in a corner, push one end of the rubber spline into the groove. Put the

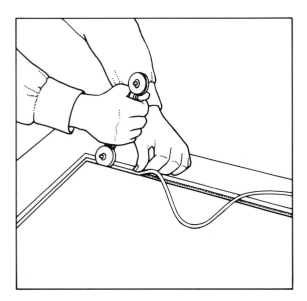

Hold the splining tool in one hand, pushing the spline forward. It works easily if you use your other hand to hold the spline ahead of the tool as you work your way around the screen frame.

concave roller on the spline and push the tool along the groove to force the spline into the groove.

When you reach the corner work the spline around the corner and continue pushing it into the groove until you have run completely around the screen. At the corner where it joins its other end, press it into the corner and then cut off the excess with a utility knife.

Trim off the excess screening material with a sharp utility knife by running the blade around the perimeter with its blade tip close to the spline.

Reinstall the screen and you have a sun shade that provides protection and lets plenty of air pass through it while keeping bugs and gnats outside.

Materials, Supplies, Tools

SunScreen screen fabric
splining installation tool
screen spline
screwdriver
pliers
measuring tape
scissors
utility knife
polish cleaner (if needed)
rags

Source

SunScreen, Phifer Wire Products
P.O. Box 1700
Tuscaloosa, AL 35403-1700
(205) 345-2120

Fabric on window treatments and furniture and carpeting are protected from the damaging rays of the sun by protective screening.

Project 44

Renovate an Old Double-Hung Window

One of the charming features of an old house is its windows. Their intricate woodwork and trim make them a focal point in a room. If they're tight and secure, you only notice them for their aesthetic value, but if they rattle and quiver in the wind, they can become a downright nuisance. Not only that, a lot of energy dollars go right out the window.

You can save the high cost of replacing an old window by installing a low-cost jamb liner or channel tracks. Available in either vinyl or metal, these tracks are designed to replace the worn outer and parting stops that no longer hold the sashes securely in the window jamb. They also replace the old rope and counterweight system. While you're doing this project don't forget to fill the air-leaking sash weight pockets on both sides of the window with insulation.

GETTING READY

Window replacement jamb liners and channels are sold in most home centers and lumberyards and are available packaged with all necessary hardware and complete installation directions. Here's how to determine what size channels are needed. Measure the height of the glass area of both the window sashes. Then measure the distance from the bottom of the jamb (the flat area that the window closes on) to the top of the jamb. Next measure the thickness of the parting stop, or the strip of wood between the windows.

If you have a very old house with windows that were built on the site, you might not be able to install jamb liners without modifying your sashes. Some old windows have sashes that are thinner than the standard $1^3/_8$-inch sash. They also might have nonstandard-size parting stops. In either case it isn't difficult to modify the sash by either gluing on a strip of wood to make the sashes thicker or changing the size of the parting stop rabbet. This, however, takes the project out of the quick-and-doable weekend category.

Jamb liners are packaged in standard lengths that fit most windows. If your windows are not a standard size, purchase a liner kit that is longer than the height of the jamb and cut it down to fit.

HERE'S HOW

Read the installation directions that come with the replacement liners thoroughly before you start this project. Then remove the window stops (the thin strips of wood that hold the inner lower sash in the jamb). You will reinstall these later, so protect them from your hammer or pry bar by placing a wide putty knife between the tool and the trim. Pry gently and work down the strip gradually. Don't pry from one end only because it causes the strip to break or splinter.

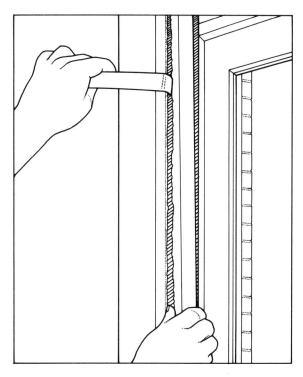

Carefully remove the parting stop from around the window with a pry bar.

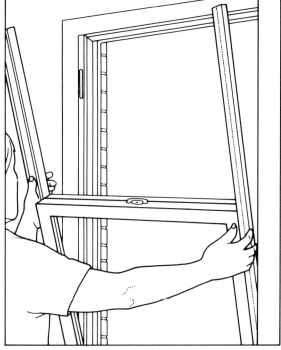

Place the replacement channels in the window opening with the sashes mounted in them.

When the window stops are removed from both sides remove the lower window sash. Be careful—it can fall out of the jamb if both sash cords are broken. Lift the sash from the jamb, remove the sash cords, and store the window in a safe place.

Remove the center parting stop by prying it out of the groove with a screwdriver or chisel. It's okay if the parting stop splinters or cracks while you're removing it because it will be replaced by the jamb liners. With the parting stop out of the way, remove the upper window sash.

Clean away any layers of paint, protruding nails, or other projections that might interfere with the installation of the jamb liners.

If you have to cut the channels to fit, trim them at the top because the bottom of each channel is precut at an angle to match the jamb.

Place the channels in position on the windowsill and push them into the window jamb. They should go in all the way and rest securely against the outer stop. Small adjustments to the jamb or channel might have to be made. When you are satisfied with the fit remove the channels from the jamb.

Now is the time to fill the counterweight pockets on the sides of the window with insulation. Remove the pulley assemblies at the top of the window jamb and then open the access panel in the side of the jamb. Use a small stick (a paint stirrer or ruler works well) to stuff as much fiberglass insulation into the cavity as you can. Pack the insulation solidly to stop the wind and air infiltration.

Install the weather stripping supplied in the kit to the top and bottom of the windows. Take special care to install the weather stripping between the windows correctly. With V-type weather stripping install the V facing down so the window operates correctly.

Installation of the new channels is easy. Place the window sashes in the channels, then rest the channels on the sill and slide the channels into the window jamb. A couple of nails or screws hold the jambs in place. Move the windows up and down to check their movement. Push the windows into final position and lock them in place. Put the inner stops in place against the jamb and check that there is free movement between them and the lower sash. The buildup of old paint might be a problem, so a little scraping and sanding could be in order. Then reinstall the stops with #4d finishing nails.

Materials, Supplies, Tools

window replacement channels
small box #4d finishing nails
#120 grit sandpaper
hammer
nailset
pry bar
6-inch-wide blade putty knife
small stick or ruler

Sources

Proseal Window Jamb Liner, Enmark Corp.
626 Armstrong Ave.
St. Paul, MN 55102
Window Fixer, Quaker City Manufacturing Co.
701 Chester Pike
Sharon Hill, PA 19079

CHAPTER EIGHT

Easy-to-Do Home Electronics Projects

Project 45

Add Your Own Telephone Extension

Since the telephone business has been deregulated by the government, you have many more choices of telephone services. One is to own your own phone. Hardware stores and home centers devote walls of merchandising space to display phones, along with every conceivable part and tool required for their successful installation. You're encouraged to do it yourself, and if you don't, your local phone company charges you to do the work. It's not as it used to be. Before all the changes in the communication business, installation and repair work was inexpensive because it was subsidized by the other company revenue, but not today. The going rate is at least $50 to $100 to have an extension phone installed.

Installing an extension phone isn't difficult, and there is little danger of electrical shock from working with phone lines. All the necessary adapters, wire, and tools are inexpensive and readily available. Rather than give specific instructions on how to run an extension phone wire from point A to point B, we'll focus on what tools, adapters, connectors, and wire to use. Then we'll suggest ideas about how to run and conceal the wire so you'll do a professional-looking job.

GETTING READY

Telephones last a long time, so unless you live in a new house or have had your phone system completely upgraded in the last ten years, chances are that at least part of your phone system is old. Older systems do not accept modern modular wiring devices, but it is a simple task to convert one since the two basic wires needed to run a phone haven't changed much in the last seventy-five years.

Most hardware stores and home centers carry everything you need to wire up an extension phone. But before you can go shopping for the right components you have to do some preliminary scouting of your phone system. What follows is how to determine the type of adapters you need and ways to run the extension wires.

HERE'S HOW

Job One is to decide where you want the new extension phone and where the nearest working phone is to that location. There is really no ideal location for an extension phone; it's wherever the phone works best for you.

Find the nearest existing phone; it doesn't have to be in the same room. It might be a phone on the other side of the wall in an adjoining room.

The illustrations suggest some possible methods of routing the thin phone wire to your extension phone. Since phone wire does not carry high voltage or heavy electrical currents, it can be safely hidden behind doors, beneath window or floor moldings, under carpet, through walls, under the house, or through the attic. You might

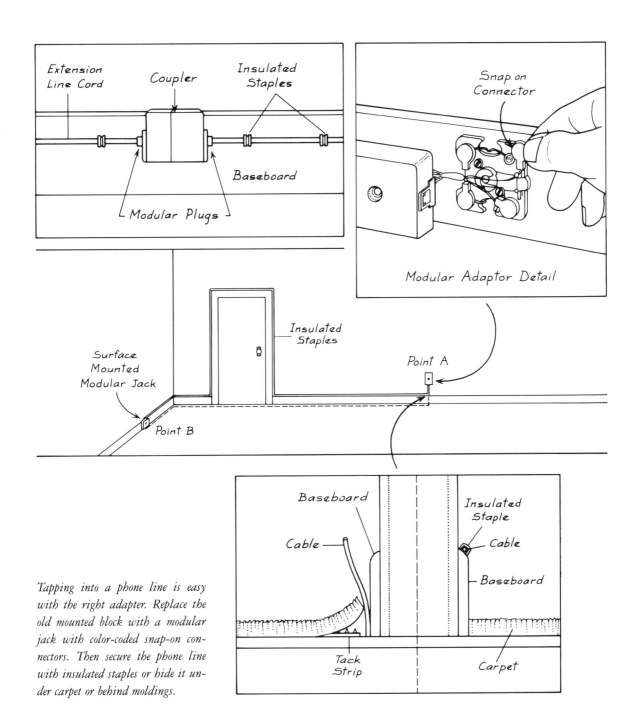

Extension Line Cord   Coupler   Insulated Staples

Baseboard

Modular Plugs

Snap on Connector

Modular Adaptor Detail

Insulated Staples

Point A

Surface Mounted Modular Jack

Point B

Baseboard

Insulated Staple

Cable

Cable

Baseboard

Tack Strip

Carpet

Tapping into a phone line is easy with the right adapter. Replace the old mounted block with a modular jack with color-coded snap-on connectors. Then secure the phone line with insulated staples or hide it under carpet or behind moldings.

find it easier to fish phone wire through a wall into a closet from another room rather than run the wire completely around the perimeter of a room.

Next, figure out how to tap into the nearest telephone line. If the phone is hooked up to a modular phone jack, then your job is an easy one. Modular jacks have a small square socket with a small notch at the bottom. The phone line is connected to the jack with a modular plug. To remove the plug all you have to do is push in on the small tab protruding from the bottom of the modular plug and pull the plug straight out of its socket.

To tap into a modular jack just remove the modular plug and insert a duplex modular jack. This adapter snaps into the single socket and provides an extra socket to plug the new extension line into.

If there is a wall plate or square box with four holes in it or if your phone is wired directly to a small square box on the wall, you have an older phone system. This isn't difficult to tap into, but you will need a screwdriver. If the plate or box has four holes in it, then purchase a cord adapter to convert the four-prong jack into a modular jack. Then connect the new extension line to one of the modular sockets on the adapter.

If your phone is wired directly to a small box, you should purchase a quick-connect modular surface-mounted modular jack. Its installation is easy. First remove the cover of the old wall box by loosening the screw in the center. You will see colored wires connected to four screw terminals. Push the snap-on clips of the new junction box on the screw heads of the old box with the same colored wires. Replace the cover of the old box and mount the new box next to the old one with the

screw provided. Then plug your extension line into the modular socket in the side of the new jack.

Making up the extension line is next. Purchase a spool of four conductor modular phone cords, a package of four conductor modular plugs, and a crimping tool. Crimping a modular plug to the end of the line is a two-step process. Insert the end of the wire into the stripping slot in the side of the tool, squeeze the tool, and remove the correct amount of outer insulation. Then push the modular plug on the end of the wire, insert the plug into the tool, and squeeze the handles to permanently attach the plug to the end of the wire.

When you're hooked up at one end of the line string the cord to the new location. The illustrations suggest some ways to hide the cord, or you can tack it to the baseboard. At the other end of the line you can install a surface-mounted modular wall jack or fish the cord up through the wall and use a modular wall jack. The wires are attached to color-coded screw terminals in the jack.

Materials, Supplies, Tools

modular phone plug crimping tool
four conductor modular plugs
surface- or wall-mounted modular wall jack
four conductor modular cords
other adapters as necessary
screwdriver

Project 46

Extend Your Television System

It's not unusual to find a TV set tucked in a corner or sitting on a shelf in more than one room of the average American household. You can get improved reception and eliminate those pesky rabbit ear antennae by hooking two TV sets to your outdoor antenna. This sounds more complicated than it is. The project involves installing a hybrid splitter, which allows you to run two sets off a single outdoor antenna. Your local hardware store has everything you need.

G E T T I N G   R E A D Y

Depending on the age of your present antenna system, the lead-in wire running from the antenna to your TV could be either a flat 300-ohm twin lead wire or a round 75-ohm coaxial (coax) cable. Either system works well if it is in good condition. In fact, there is actually less signal loss per foot with the older 300-ohm twin lead wire. The biggest problem with the twin lead wire is that it is not shielded and can pick up noise, which you see as interference on the TV screen from nearby house wiring. This can also be due to pipes or other metal objects it might run parallel to. For this reason coax cable is preferred for running around the house to different TV sets. Most of the modern splitters, filters, and amplifiers are also designed to work with this type of cable.

It is easy to make the switch from a flat wire system to coax. There are several different types of transformers that allow you to connect 75-ohm coax cable to a 300-ohm flat lead line. The best place to do this is at the antenna, but if you don't relish roof work, you can install the transformer anywhere in the line. Purchase an outdoor transformer if connections will be made outside. From this point on you can use coax cable.

For this project we explain how to make up the cables and where to install the splitter. The logistics route depends on many variables, most importantly the location of the sets in your house. You'll have to do some scouting around or under your house to decide the best route to get the cable from set to set. One of the easiest routes we know is running the antenna-down lead into the basement or crawl space first and from there split the cable to hook up to several rooms.

Television antenna and cable television installers think nothing of running the coax cable around the outside of a house. They take the direct approach and punch through the wall wherever an outlet is needed. This might provide the easiest access, but it's not exactly the most attractive one, having the outside of your house look as if it's wrapped in wire. We think it's well worth the effort to try to somehow run the cable inside the house.

Spend some time walking around your house and looking at the wires already there. It's not a

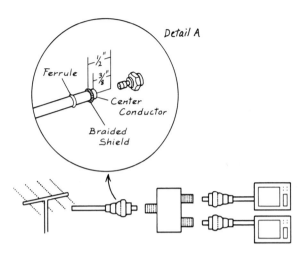

Detail A

Ferrule

Center
Conductor

Braided
Shield

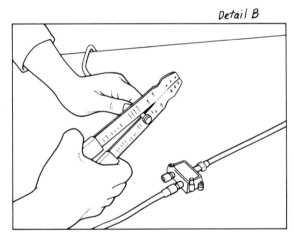

Detail B

A hybrid splitter installed in the lead-in wire from a roof-mounted antenna allows two TV sets to share the antenna. Prepare coaxial cable (detail A). Slide the ferrule up snug against the fitting and crimp it tight by placing the ferrule in the crimping tool and squeezing down hard on the handles (detail B).

bad idea to make a mental note of which wires (telephone, utility lines) run where.

HERE'S HOW

Look at the antenna and follow the wires to see where they go. If you have twin lead wires coming down from the antenna, install an indoor/outdoor 300-to-75-ohm matching transformer on the end of the twin lead. From then on use 75-ohm coaxial cable.

Coaxial cable comes with a male F screw fitting at each end. As soon as you cut the cable to the length that you need, you have to install a fitting on the other end to connect the cable to the splitter or TV set. Installing a F type connector is easy; it just takes a little patience. You'll find a wiring diagram printed on the connector package that's similar to our illustration.

Before you begin preparing the end of the cable to receive the F connector, slip the ferrule (small ring) on the cable and slide it down the wire so it's out of the way. After the connector is in place crimp this ferrule over the fitting to lock it in place.

Next strip $\frac{1}{2}$ inch of the outer insulation off the end of the cable. Unravel the braided wire or foil surrounding the center conductor and bend it back over the outer insulation. Trim $\frac{3}{8}$ inch of the insulation surrounding the center conductor off to bare the wire. Slip the fitting over the center conductor and push it as far as it goes. Check that the outer braided wire is still folded back over the outer insulation, so you can work the body of the fitting under the braid. Keep twisting the fitting to help it slide under the braid until the braided wire is in contact with the front of the fitting. Trim away the excess wire but be careful not to cut through the outer insulation. Then slip the ferrule over the fitting and crimp it tight with a cable crimping tool. This sounds involved but it really takes just a few minutes once you get the hang of it.

You don't need much help installing the splitter. It's as simple as attaching the lead-in cable for the antenna to the terminal marked IN on the splitter. Connect the other cables that will lead to the TV sets to the terminals marked OUT.

At the back of each television set you should connect the end of the coax cable to the IN terminal of the transformer/splitter. Attach a short piece of flat 300-ohm wire to the screw terminals marked VHF on the splitter, then attach the other end to the VHF antenna terminals on your set. Do the same on the UHF side of the splitter, and the set is ready to use.

Materials, Supplies, Tools

1 indoor/outdoor matching transformer 300/75 ohm
1 50-foot length of RG59U coaxial cable
1 box male F screw-type coax fittings
1 75-ohm input/2 75-ohm outputs—hybrid splitter
2 transformer/signal splitter—75-ohm input/300-ohm outputs
crimping tool

Project 47

Install a Security Device

Sad to say, but it doesn't take more than reading the headlines of your local newspaper to make you concerned about the security of your home. That alone has made the home security business a growth industry. As electronic gadgets become increasingly smaller and less expensive, companies are able to manufacture inexpensive wireless security systems that can be easily installed by the average homeowner.

These systems are easy to install because most of them use small radio transmitters to link a remote intrusion sensor to a main control unit instead of running wires. These transmitters can be wired to several sensors and can be mounted in unobtrusive areas.

With this type of system all you have to deal with are the short wires leading from the sensors at the doors and windows and the transmitter. That's what this project is all about—hiding the wires to make a security system barely noticeable. You can cut a mortise for the magnetic sensor and drill a concealment hole for sensor wires that will make the job look like a professional installation. And it takes less than thirty minutes of additional time at each door or window and some clever carpentry skills you can quickly master.

We installed a wireless system called REFLEX manufactured by Heath/Zenith, which uses small magnetic door/window sensors. These sensors have two parts: a switch body with a set of thin wires attached to it and a movable magnet. The body of the sensor is mounted on the door frame or window casing and the magnet goes on the door or window sash. If either is opened the magnet moves away from the sensor body and the internal switch opens, alerting the transmitter.

To make the installation look neater and be less obtrusive, we installed the body of the sensor in a shallow mortise in the door or window casing. Then we drilled a hole through the casing to route the wires through the casing. To do this you need a sharp $1/4$-inch wood chisel and a $3/8$-inch in diameter electrician's drill bit that is 8 inches or longer. Everything else is supplied by the manufacturer.

Each security system comes with a complete installation manual. The carpentry tricks we're suggesting will work with any system that uses magnetic sensors. Follow the installation manual provided with the system you chose. After you have everything planned out and all the modules are working then go back and conceal the wires.

H E R E ' S   H O W

To install a magnetic sensor and route the wires to the transmitter here's what's involved. Locate and check the function of the sensor and the system and mark its location on the door or window casing. Trace around its perimeter with a sharp pencil and then remove the sensor.

With a sharp ¼-inch wood chisel remove the wood from the outlined area to a depth of about ⅛ inch. First make a series of parallel, closely spaced cuts down the length of the outline. Try to make the cuts the same depth. Then go back and remove the wood chips and smooth the bottom of the mortise.

Place the body of the sensor in the mortise and check its fit. Adjust the depth of the mortise so the sensor is straight. Then drill a ⅜-inch hole through the door or window casing, beginning in the center of the mortise. Thread the sensor wires through the hole and push the sensor body into position in the mortise. You may have to chisel out some more wood in the center of the mortise to make room for the wires so they can pass under the sensor. Put the sensor back in position and use it as a template to drill the pilot holes for the mounting screws. Then secure the sensor with the screws provided.

Install the magnet half of the sensor opposite the sensor body on the door or window sash. This magnet must be mounted on the movable part of a door or window and be moved far enough from the sensor body to open the switch when the door or window is opened wide enough for someone to pass. Install it with the screws or self-sticking foam strips provided.

Lead the sensor wires along the top of the door or window casing and hold them in place with insulated staples placed every six inches or so.

You can attach several sensors to a single transmitter. Splice on longer wires to the leads of the sensor switches and then route the wires along the top of the door or window casing, over or behind cabinets, or even behind the baseboard.

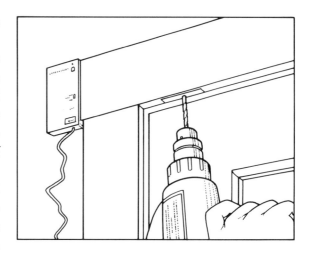

Use an 8-inch-long ⅜-inch drill bit to drill the hole to run the sensor wires through the window or door molding so the wires can be concealed.

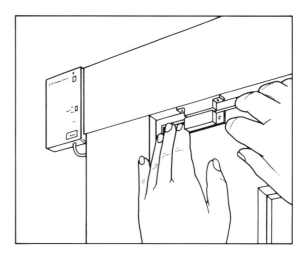

The transmitter and sensor are less obtrusive if you conceal the wiring. The sensor body contains the switch, and the magnet half of the sensing unit is mounted on the movable part of the door or window. All wires are concealed by routing them through the door casing.

The time spent concealing the wires will be paid back by creating a clean-looking area without a lot of wires running across the woodwork.

Materials, Supplies, Tools

motion sensor, receiver unit
8-inch-long $^3/_8$-inch drill bit
electric drill
measuring tape
$^1/_4$-inch wood chisel

Source

REFLEX Wireless Supervised Home Protection
System, Heath Zenith Co.
Hilltop Rd.
St. Joseph, MI 49085
(616) 429-5499

Install a Low-Voltage Outdoor Light

With the advent of low-voltage outdoor lighting it's possible at a relatively low cost to light up your yard. Low-voltage technology makes installing an outdoor light an easy do-it-yourself project and one that's safe because there's no danger of receiving a shock.

A transformer reduces your regular 120-volt household current to a safe 12 volts. From the transformer current is carried to a low-voltage light fixture by a weather-resistant cable that doesn't have to be buried under ground. These fixtures come in a variety of styles to light up yards, walkways, decks, and patios.

If you've never done an electrical project, this is a good one because it's easy to install a few lights on your deck or patio or run a string of them down a walkway. We explain all the basics you need to know to get started—your job is to supply the imagination.

GETTING READY

Low-voltage lighting is sold in starter kits that include everything you need. The transformer is capable of powering more than a few lights, so you can extend the basic system at a later date to include additional lights.

These transformers have a maximum wattage rating, and you can use it to calculate how many lights the transformer can power. Most fixtures use bulbs that consume about 11 watts. Divide 11 into the power rating of the transformer to find the number of lights you can run off that transformer. Even though we suggest you start with a modest system, allow for future expansion.

While you are looking at transformers, decide the type of control that you want. All the transformers have on and off switches, but some have photoelectric eyes that can turn the lights on at dusk and off at dawn. Some transformers also have timers, while others offer a combination photo switch and timer.

The starter kits come with 16-gauge cable that is adequate for cable runs of up to 100 feet. Unlike 120-volt wiring there is considerable voltage drop along this 12-volt direct current line. The lights will light up at the end of a long cable run but they will not burn brightly. If you are installing lights with runs up to 150 feet from the transformer, use heavier 14-gauge cable. Use 12-gauge cable for longer runs up to 200 feet.

HERE'S HOW

Each manufacturer supplies complete planning and installation booklets with its products. They all are installed in basically the same way. Here is a general rundown of what it takes to get a simple system up and running.

The first thing you should know is that work-

Some transformers that convert 120-volt house current into 12 volts have built-in timers and photoelectric eyes that turn the light on at dusk and off at dawn.

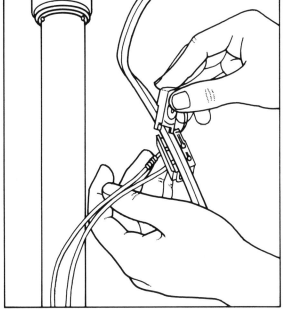

Installing a low-voltage light to the cable is easy. Place the cable in the special tap, then close the tap over the cable and snap it shut. Small prongs in the tap penetrate the cable insulation to make contact with the cable conductors.

Light up walkways in the yard to assure safe footing and provide attractive accent lighting. This system can be installed in a couple of hours.

ing with a 12-volt system is safe. But it's still electricity, so you must maintain polarity (hook the same wires to the same terminals through the system) and pay attention to how you hook up the fixtures.

Start the installation by attaching the cable to the transformer. The transformer has two terminal screws. Loosen them and attach one side of the low voltage cable to each screw terminal. If there are no spade fittings on the end of the cable, strip off about an inch of insulation from each conductor. Twist the wire strands of one conductor together to form a single wire and wrap it clockwise around the terminal screw. Hook up the other conductor in the same way. Plug the transformer into a grounded outlet and turn it on.

Next position the light fixtures where you want them. Unless your ground is unusually hard, you can push the fixture's ground stake into the earth by hand. Otherwise dig a hole for the stake. Don't beat on the fixture—it's made of plastic and can't take too much abuse.

Next determine the best way to lead the cable from the transformer to the lights. Don't cover it—just lay it out on the ground where you think it will eventually go. Remember that you can tap into the wire later to add lights (up to the capacity of the transformer) at any time.

Hook the fixtures up to the cable. Most systems have a clamp on tap with prongs that push through the insulation to make the connection. Installing a light is as simple as laying the cable in the tap and closing the tap around the cable. You will know right away if everything is working because the fixture will turn on as soon as it is connected.

When everything is wired up and working, go back and hide the cable. It doesn't have to be buried; you might conceal it under the base of bushes or shrubbery or cover it with mulch or ground cover. If you decide to bury it in the lawn, make a slit in the sod with a spade held at a 45-degree angle. Then push the cable into the slit and step on the ground to close the cut.

Materials, Supplies, Tools

low-voltage deck light
cable
transformer
wire snippers
screwdriver
garden spade

Source

Malibu Compact Deck Light, Intermatic Inc.
Intermatic Plaza
Spring Grove, IL 60081-9698

CHAPTER NINE

Projects for
the
Great Outdoors

Project 49

Make a Window Flower Box

Long before there were books for apartment and condominium dwellers about "container gardening," there were those of us who, for whatever reason, got more enjoyment from digging in a window box than in Mother Earth herself. A simple window box filled with colorful flowers can easily and inexpensively decorate a house. You can drive by the same house all winter long and never notice it until one spring morning it seems to come alive with window boxes spilling over with purple petunias. And the eye-catcher of a group of high-rise balconies is the one that's outlined with ivy and bright red geraniums.

Today you can buy window boxes made of plastic, pottery, and wood and in sizes to fit just about any window. But for a few dollars and an afternoon in the workshop you can build your own redwood window box for use indoors or outdoors.

G E T T I N G   R E A D Y

The box in the illustration measures 37½ inches overall and is made of readily available lumber. We used redwood with 1 × 6s for the bottom and front and 1 × 8s for the back and end pieces. Because some of the pieces required are short, you might find scrap lumber at the lumberyard to use.

Use only galvanized fasteners or aluminum nails to hold the box together. Redwood holds up, but if the nails begin to rust they will cause un-

sightly stains on the wood, and eventually the rust stains will begin to show on your house siding.

If you want a colorful window box that's not in a natural wood shade, then consider making it with pressure-treated wood. It is less expensive than redwood and will last just as long. Also we suggest a stain rather than paint. A heavy-bodied stain covers like paint but usually doesn't peel or chip like paint.

H E R E ' S   H O W

This is a good first-time woodworking project for someone who likes to garden as well. Cut the back, bottom, and front to length. Use #6d galvanized or aluminum box nails to attach the back to the bottom. Drive the nails partially through the back so their points just begin to stick out the other side. Align the end of the bottom and back and then nail them together. Nail the front to the bottom in the same way.

Cut the ends into 7¼-inch squares. Along one of the end grain sides measure in 1 inch from the corner and make a mark. Then from the opposite corner measure up 5¾ inches and mark this spot on the end. Connect these points with a line and then cut away the small triangular part with a fine-tooth saw (see illustration). Use this end as a pattern to make the other. Then nail both of the parts to the end of the box.

There are many ways to hang the box. Proba-

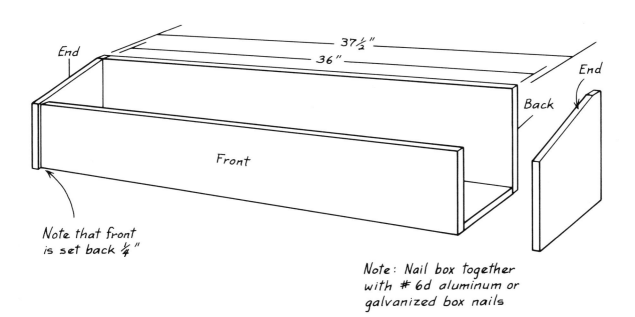

End

End

Back

$37\frac{1}{2}''$

$36''$

Front

Note that front is set back $\frac{1}{4}''$

Note: Nail box together with # 6d aluminum or galvanized box nails

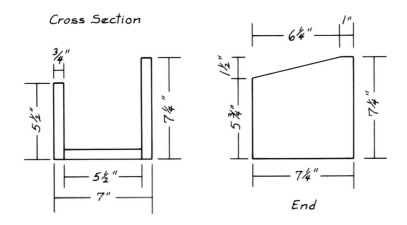

Cross Section

$\frac{3}{4}''$

$5\frac{1}{2}''$

$7\frac{1}{4}''$

$5\frac{1}{2}''$

$7''$

$6\frac{1}{4}''$

$1''$

$1\frac{1}{2}''$

$5\frac{3}{4}''$

$7\frac{1}{4}''$

$7\frac{1}{4}''$

End

165

PARTS LIST			
NAME	AMOUNT	SIZE	MATERIAL
Bottom	1	$3/4'' \times 5^{1}/2'' \times 36''$	pine
Back	1	$3/4'' \times 7^{1}/4'' \times 36''$	pine
Front	1	$3/4'' \times 5^{1}/2'' \times 36''$	pine
End	2	$3/4'' \times 7^{1}/4'' \times 7^{1}/4''$	pine

bly the easiest is to screw it directly to the front edge of the windowsill. Use at least four $1^{3}/4$-inch #8 brass screws per box. Another option, if you want to mount the box on a railing, is to use a U bolt. This is a U-shaped bolt with both of the legs threaded. Drill holes for the two legs through the back of the box and then slip the U bolt over the railing. Push it through the holes in the box and install the washers and nuts. Once it's tightened the box is securely clamped to the railing.

Fill it with your favorite flowers and you've created a masterpiece!

Materials, Supplies, Tools

1 7-foot 1 × 6 pine
1 6-foot 1 × 8 pine
4 $1^{3}/4$-inch #8 flathead brass screws
small box #6d galvanized or aluminum box
  nails
handsaw
hammer
screwdriver
measuring tape
drill and drill bits
wood stain
paintbrush
pencil

Project 50

Make a Concrete Foundation for a Storage Shed

Until you live in a house without a basement and garage, you don't realize just how much "stuff" is acquired (and necessary) for working around the house and in the yard. Where do you store the lawn mower, snow shovel, garden equipment, and extension ladder, not to mention the gas grill and bicycles?

The old garden shed comes to the rescue, but today it's not the frumpy utilitarian box that previewed in the early sixties. The nineties offer a wide range of styles, sizes, and prices. There are metal sheds made of 100 percent galvanized steel, while others feature an upgraded protective coating; the latest edition of vinyl-clad steel buildings are designed with spacious interiors and attractive exteriors.

These outbuildings are assembled in basically the same way, with numerous parts that fit together and are fastened with nuts, bolts, and screws. Because of this, a power screwdriver and socket wrench ratchet set will speed the job considerably. Choose a day when the ground is dry and not muddy, and don't tackle this project on a windy day when some of the large, lightweight panels might catch the wind and go sailing off. Calm and dry are the weather watchwords for this project.

One of the biggest problems with these lightweight buildings is keeping them in place in high winds or storms. You can anchor them with tie-down kits provided by the manufacturer, but a concrete slab is by far the best base. Constructing a slab for a storage shed is a lot of work, but it's not impossible for a do-it-yourselfer. Ready-mix concrete makes this a simple project. You can dig, frame up, pour, and finish an average-size slab in a weekend. By the following weekend it's ready for the shed.

GETTING READY

The best location for a shed depends on several factors. It should be built where its access is convenient. The ground should be level and have good drainage. If your site slopes and there is more than a couple of inches' difference in elevation, consider hiring someone to build the slab. You can do it but it's more of a trick to level the forms on a sloping site. Close to where you plan to erect the shed, place a 16-foot-long 2 × 4 on the ground and then place a carpenter's level on it. Move the board up and down until the bubble in the level is centered. If one end of the board is off the ground more than an inch or so, stop and call for help.

Consult the assembly booklet for the required size of the foundation slab. Unless you are erecting a very large shed, four 16-foot 2 × 4s are all you need to make the forms. You will also need to purchase enough crushed stone to cover the bottom of the foundation excavation to a 4-inch depth.

Make arrangements to have the stone deliv-

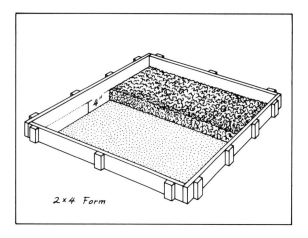

After building the form and removing the sod, fill with 4 inches of gravel before you fill the form with concrete.

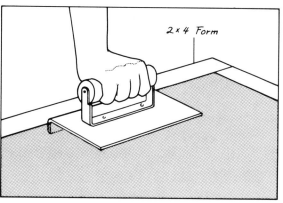

Rent an edging tool to round over the outside edges of the slab to prevent the concrete from chipping and to give the slab a finished look.

Rest a straight 2×4 on the form and then work it back and forth across the top of the form to level the concrete. This is called "striking off."

ered, since it's too heavy to fool with in the trunk of your car. Depending on how your lumberyard sells stone, figure 1 cubic foot of stone will cover 3 square feet of a 4-inch-thick slab. Order a little less than you think you'll need unless you have a use for leftover stones.

Check with your local building department to see if you need a building permit for this job. You must observe all property line setback requirements, so the position of the shed is a consideration. The building inspector might want to see the forms with the stone in them before you fill it with concrete.

HERE'S HOW

Construction of the form for a small slab like this on level ground is simple. The main thing to keep in mind is that everything must be right before the concrete is poured. You use the top of the form as a guide when finishing the concrete so it has to be level.

There are many ways to lay out a small slab. The way we do it is to first make the form, then position it on the site and excavate the dirt, and finally level and square it up.

When making the form remember that it is the inside dimensions of the form that are important. Cut the 2 × 4 ends to the exact width of the slab. Cut the 2 × 4 for the sides equal to the length of the slab plus 3 inches (the thickness of the side 2 × 4s).

Nail the sides to the ends with #16d common nails. Put the form in place and check the position. When you are satisfied that the form is in the correct location, use a spade with a sharp, flat blade to remove the sod inside the form.

Cut the sod into strips about a foot wide to reuse in another part of the yard. Simply cut the sod with the spade, pry up a corner, and work the blade under the grass to cut the roots about 3 inches down. Roll or fold the sod and keep it moist.

With the sod removed you should have a depression about 2 to 3 inches deep. Now go back and level up the form to make sure that it is square. The easiest way to do this is to find the high corner by setting a carpenter's level on the length (the long side) of the form; the bubble will point to the high end of the board. Then place the level in the center of the end (the short side) at the high end. The bubble in the level will again point to the high side. Mark this corner, then go to the other length (the long side opposite the one you placed your level on before) and place the level on the form. The bubble should point to the same end. This might not be the case if the ground is level. If the form is only out of level by a 1/4 inch or so, you probably won't see any big changes in the level bubble as you move it around. In this case the form is okay the way it sits.

If you do find a high side, use the spade to scoop a little dirt out from under the form and recheck to see if it's level. Take the dirt out slowly—you should remove no more than an inch or so. Keep checking the form until it is level.

Next, square up the form by measuring the distance between opposite corners. If they are the same, then the form is square. If they are not, use a rafter square to help square up the corners and remeasure.

When the form is square cut a dozen or so stakes from the scrap 2 × 4 cutoffs. If your ground is hard, make the stakes from 2 × 2 stock because the smaller stakes are easier to drive into the ground. Make the ends pointed by cutting through the boards at an angle. Each cut makes two stakes.

Drive stakes outside the form, butting them snug against it to anchor it in place. Then drive a nail through the form into the stake to lock the form to it.

Lay a 16-foot 2 × 4 across the sides of the form so it sits on top of it. Move the board over the form to check the depth of the excavation. Note that there should be 7 to 8 inches between the bottom of this board and the ground. If not, remove some dirt to make it that way. But if the depth is greater, don't fill in the low spots with dirt; you should use stone for fill-in material instead. Then spread the stone subbase evenly and to a uniform depth of about 3 to 4 inches. Recheck everything, and your form is ready to fill.

Let your fingers do the walking and call a ready-mix concrete company and arrange for delivery. Tell them the size of the slab and that it will be 4 inches thick; they will tell you how much concrete to order. Ready-mix companies have a minimum order or levy a delivery charge if an order is small, so you might have to pay for more concrete than you will actually use. The truck will unload only what you need.

Unless the truck can get close to the form, you'll have to transport the concrete in a wheelbarrow. Concrete trucks are very heavy and their tires make deep ruts in the lawn if the ground is at all soft. So it's best to plan on hauling the concrete with a wheelbarrow. If you don't have one, you can rent one for a few dollars a day.

Filling the form is a lot of muscle work but not complicated. Either have the truck direct the delivery chute into the form or transport the concrete mix to the form in the wheelbarrow. Use a rake to spread the concrete as it begins to fill. Work the rake back and forth to push the concrete into the corners and fill any voids at the bottom of the form.

When the form is full take your 16-foot 2 × 4 and place it across the form. Work it back and forth across the form to strike off or level the concrete. Drag it down the form to level the concrete as you go.

When you reach the other end the concrete should be level with the top of the form. The 2 × 4 produces a rough-textured finish that is adequate for the floor of a storage shed. If you want a smoother finish, wait until the water sheen leaves the surface of the concrete, and then use a metal trowel to further smooth the surface of the concrete. Then follow with an edging tool to slightly round the outside corners of the slab.

When you are satisfied with the finish, cover the slab with a sheet of plastic and leave it alone. If the weather is hot, remove the plastic a few times during the week and wet the slab to help it cure properly.

In a week it will be ready to build on. Most metal buildings are secured to a concrete slab with lead concrete anchors and bolts that you can purchase with the shed. Check the assembly manual for specific directions about securing the building to the foundation.

Materials, Supplies, Tools	Source
4 16-foot 2 × 4 pine stock	Arrow Steel Storage Buildings
crushed stone	100 Alexander Ave.
concrete	Pompton Plains, NJ 07444
2 pounds #16d common nails	
hammer	
carpenter's level	
tape measure	
rafter square	
garden rake	
concrete edging tool (rent)	
spade	
handsaw	
metal trowel	
sheet of plastic	

Project 51

Make a Tile House-Number Board

Is there anything more annoying than driving down a dark street trying to find the house numbers on someone's house? Our colorful tile house-number board makes your house clearly identifiable and is an attractive enhancement to your house's exterior.

We made a wood frame for white ceramic tiles decorated with a colorful design and numeral. Order the numeral tiles that you need from a tile retailer. The tiles feature black numbers with several colors and designs for you to choose from.

Any type of wood can be used to frame the numerals. If the house-number board will be exposed to the elements, choose from cedar, redwood, or pressure-treated wood. Use a water sealer to protect the wood. If the number board is mounted under a protective eave or overhang, you can use painted or polyurethane-sealed pine.

Wherever it's mounted make certain that the house numbers are clearly visible from the street and that in the evening there's a light to illuminate them.

GETTING READY

The size of the back and side trim is determined by the size of the tiles. We used decorative tiles with bold black numerals that measured 4 inches by 8 inches. When you shop for materials purchase the tiles first, then select the wood.

If you find tiles that are different sizes than the ones we used, adjust the parts to fit. The back is the same size as the tiles laid side by side. The top and bottom trim are the same length as the back, and the end trim parts are $1/2$ inch longer than the width of the back to allow for the thickness of the other trim parts.

Once you have the materials assembled this is a quickie project. It's also a good primer for a larger tiling project like adding a tile backsplash in the kitchen or tiling the foyer floor. So if you want to experiment in working with tile, this is a good project for you.

HERE'S HOW

Lay out the tile numerals and cut the back to size so it fits them. Then cut the top and bottom trim to the exact length of the back. Apply glue to the top edge of the back and then put the top trim in place and nail it to the back with four or five evenly spaced #3d finishing nails. Install the bottom trim in the same way, checking that both parts are flush with the ends of the back.

Remeasure the width of the back trim assembly and cut the side trim parts long enough to cover the ends of the top and bottom trim. Then glue and nail the side trim parts to each end.

If you plan to paint, stain, or finish the frame, do it before you install the tiles. We recommend that you give the frame a coat of wood sealer and then a coat of wipe-on oil finish if it will not be directly exposed to the weather. Use an exterior gloss paint if it will be exposed to the weather.

Put the tiles into the frame for a test fit and then remove them. Apply a liberal bead of acrylic adhesive caulking to the back of the first tile. Run the bead around the perimeter of the tile about $\frac{1}{2}$ inch from its edge and then run an **X**-shaped bead in the tile center. Push the tile in place and work it back and forth to spread the adhesive caulking in back. Repeat this process for the other tiles.

The easiest way to hang the frame is to attach a couple of brass picture hangers to the back and then screw the brackets to the exterior siding of the house.

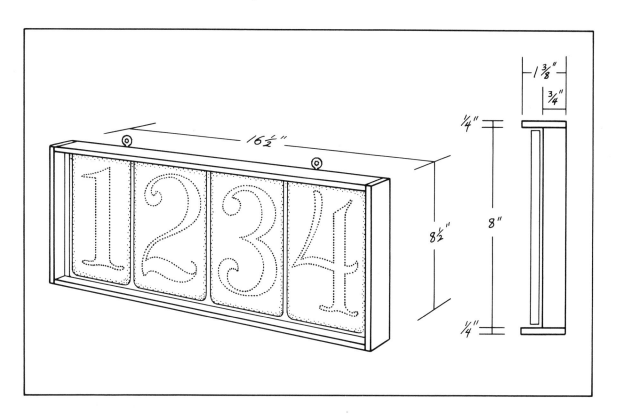

PARTS LIST

NAME	AMOUNT	SIZE	MATERIAL
Back	1	$3/4'' \times 8'' \times 16''$	pine
Side trim	2	$1/4'' \times 1 3/8'' \times 16''$	pine
End trim	2	$1/4'' \times 1 3/8'' \times 8 1/2''$	pine
Tile numbers	4	$1/2'' \times 4'' \times 8''$	ceramic tile

Materials, Supplies, Tools

decorative tiles with numerals
1 8-by-16-inch (scrap) $3/4''$ AC exterior ply-
    wood
1 6-foot $1 3/8$-inch lattice
2 1-inch brass hangers
1 tube acrylic latex adhesive caulking
small bottle carpenter's glue
small box #3d galvanized finishing nails
wipe-on oil finish, wood sealer, or exterior gloss
    paint
paintbrush
hammer
nailset
hand or circular saw
screwdriver

Source

Decorative house-number tiles
Summitville Tiles, Inc.
Summitville, OH 43962
(216) 223-1511

Build a Slatted Garden Bench

As soon as you start using this bench, you'll wonder how on earth you got along without it. Use it in the backyard for a resting place or as a coffee table in front of deck chairs. Make two for the breezeway to display a collection of clay pots filled with flowers.

We designed the bench to be built out of pressure-treated lumber, either redwood or cedar. Since only straight cuts are necessary, the bench doesn't require serious carpentry skills or tools. Cutting the lumber to length will take the most time, but after that assembling it will move along quite easily. When it's all together apply a protective coating with a water seal (such as Thompson's) for mildew resistance.

G E T T I N G   R E A D Y

The easiest way to get the 14 2 × 4s that you need is to have the lumberyard cut seven 8-foot boards in half. These parts don't have to be precisely 48 inches long but they should all be the same length. This bench is designed to be exposed to the weather, so you should use only aluminum or galvanized nails.

H E R E ' S   H O W

Cut the 2 × 4 seat slats and the cleats to length. Lay them on edge next to one another and arrange them for best color and grain match. Turn them over and align them at one end. Draw a layout line across each end of the bundle 7½ inches in from the end. Lay a cleat on the line and place it on the side of the line toward the center of the seat.

Then nail the cleat to the slats. Start at the first slat and drive two #16d galvanized nails through the cleat into the slats. Push the next slat tight against the first, align the ends, and nail it to the cleat with one #16d nail. Then drive three or four evenly spaced #8d common aluminum or galvanized nails through the side of the second slat into the first. Nail the next slat to the cleat with two #16d nails, then use #8d nails on the sides. Alternate this nailing pattern until all the slats are in place. Check the alignment at both ends and then install the other cleat in the same way.

Cut the braces and legs to length. Align the end of the brace and cleat together and then nail the brace to the side of the cleat. Do this to the other side of the cleat and then place a leg between the braces. Align the leg so that it is set back 1½ inches from the end of the brace. Check that it is square with the cleat and then nail it in place by driving nails through the braces into the leg. Install the leg at the other end in the same way and then go to the other end of the bench and repeat the sequence.

Turn the bench over and sand the raw edges of the slats to a slight radius to prevent splinters. Then give the bench a coat of sealer, and it's ready to use.

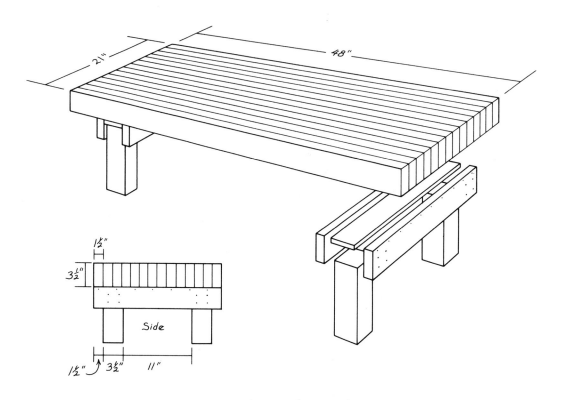

Side

Materials, Supplies, Tools

8 8-foot 2 × 4 redwood/pressure-treated wood   1 pint water sealer
1 8-foot 2 × 6 redwood/pressure-treated wood   hammer
1 5-foot 4 × 4 redwood/pressure-treated wood   square
2 pounds #16d galvanized nails   hand or circular saw
2 pounds #8d galvanized nails   paintbrush
3 sheets #120 grit abrasive paper

PARTS LIST			
NAME	AMOUNT	SIZE	MATERIAL
Slat	14	1½″ × 3½″ × 48″	redwood
Cleat	2	1½″ × 3½″ × 21″	redwood
Brace	4	1½″ × 5½″ × 21″	redwood
Leg	4	3½″ × 3½″ × 11″	redwood